History of Judaism
The Next Ten Years

BROWN UNIVERSITY
BROWN JUDAIC STUDIES

Edited by

Jacob Neusner
Wendell S. Dietrich, Ernest S. Frerichs,
Horst R. Moehring, Sumner B. Twiss

Board of Editors

David Altshuler, George Washington University
David R. Blumenthal, Emory University
Baruch M. Bokser, University of California, Berkeley
Joel Gereboff, Arizona State University
Robert Goldenberg, State University of New York, Stony Brook
David Goodblatt, Haifa University
William Scott Green, University of Rochester
Peter Haas, Vanderbilt University
Martin Jaffee, University of Virginia
Shamai Kanter, Temple Beth El, Rochester, New York
Jack N. Lightstone, Concordia University
Irving Mandelbaum, University of Texas
Alan J. Peck, Brown University
Gary G. Porton, University of Illinois
Charles Primus, University of Notre Dame
Marc L. Raphael, Ohio State University
Richard S. Sarason, Hebrew Union College-Jewish Institute of Religion
Tzvee Zahavy, University of Minnesota

Roger Brooks
Louis Newman

Number 21

History of Judaism
The Next Ten Years

by Baruch M. Bokser

History of Judaism
The Next Ten Years

by
Baruch M. Bokser

Scholars Press

Distributed by
SCHOLARS PRESS
101 Salem Street
Chico, CA 95926

History of Judaism
The Next Ten Years

by

Baruch M. Bokser

Copyright ©1980
Brown University

Library of Congress Cataloging in Publication Data

Max Richter Conversation on the History of Judaism,
  5th Providence, 1980.
    History of Judaism, the next ten years.

  (Brown Judaic studies ; no. 21)
    Papers presented at the Fifth Max Richter Conversation on the History of Judaism, Providence, R.I., June 23–24, 1980.
    Includes bibliographical references and index.
    1. Judaism—Historiography—Congresses. 2. Philosophy, Jewish—Congresses. 3. Philosophy, Medieval—Congresses. I. Bokser, Baruch M. II. Brown University. III. Title. IV. Series.
BM30.M38 1980   296'.09   80-25501
ISBN 0-89130-450-9
ISBN 0-89130-451-7 (pbk.)

Printed in the United States of America
1 2 3 4 5
McNaughton & Gunn
Ann Arbor, Michigan 48106

For Leonard Lesko

TABLE OF CONTENTS

PREFACE ix
ABBREVIATIONS xi
INTRODUCTION xiii
   Baruch M. Bokser, University of California, Berkeley

PART ONE: JUDAISM IN ANCIENT TIMES

I.   Story as History in Ancient Judaism: Formulating Fresh Questions 3
     Jacob Neusner, Brown University

II. Towards the Rehabilitation of Talmudic History . . . 31
     David Goodblatt, University of Haifa

III. A New Approach to Early Jewish Prayer 45
     Tzvee Zahavy, University of Minnesota

PART TWO: JUDAISM IN MEDIEVAL TIMES

IV. Some Remarks on the Study of Jewish Philosophy in the Middle Ages 63
     Aviezer Ravitzky, Hebrew University

V.   On Studying Philosophic Mysticism 81
     David Blumenthal, Emory University

PART THREE: JUDAISM IN MODERN TIMES

VI. The History of Judaism in Poland in 1750-1815 and the Sources of Anti-Modernization 95
     Hillel Levine, Yale University

VII. The Uses of Social Theory in the Study of Modern Judaism 117
     Arnold Eisen, Columbia University

INDEX 133

PREFACE AND ACKNOWLEDGEMENTS

This volume contains seven papers in the history of Judaism. The authors explain what problem presently challenges them, why they believe it urgent for them to pursue it, and how their agenda and methods compare with those of previous scholarship. The papers by Professors David Goodblatt, Tzvee Zahavy, Aviezer Ravitzky, David Blumenthal, Hillel Levine, and Arnold Eisen were presented at the Fifth Max Richter Conversation on the History of Judaism, Providence, R.I., June 23-24, 1980. A seventh paper delivered there, "Reading and Writing of Rabbinism: Towards an Interpretation of Rabbinic Literature," by Professor William Scott Green, will be published elsewhere. An additional paper, by Professor Jacob Neusner, has been included because it takes up the overall challenge and appropriately belongs with the other essays. It serves to set the stage for the other papers.

The editor and the participants remain indebted to the Max Richter Foundation for funding the conference and for the typing and production of this book. Max Richter enjoyed conversation in which individuals in a quiet manner could exchange their views. The annual Max Richter Conversations have provided such a context. At the fifth conference, at which these papers were delivered, the participants had ample opportunity to discuss with each author the presentations and critically to reflect upon the issues. The editor's introduction has been greatly shaped by the remarks made in those discussions.

The papers are printed essentially in the form in which they were delivered. While in the aforementioned question-and-answer portion of the sessions, the authors may have further clarified their comments, the original statements have an integrity of their own and hence are published in that form. As editor, I have made slight stylistic changes to clarify the exposition and format changes to standardize the structure of the book. But I have not sought to standardize other matters such as transliteration preferences.

I am appreciative of the authors' cooperation in the preparation of the manuscript. I am especially thankful to several colleagues. Professors Jacob Neusner and William Scott Green graciously gave of their time to discuss the organization of the volume and the contents of the Introduction. Professors Howard Smith, David Winston, and Wilhelm Wuellner offered critical comments on several matters.

History of Judaism

    I remain indebted to the University of California, Berkeley, for providing me with a context in which I can pursue my own research in the history of Judaism in ancient times. I am appreciative of my colleagues' interest in and support for my studies. Professor Leonard Lesko, Chairman of the Department of Near Eastern Studies, in particular has taken personal interest in my research and field, and I dedicate this volume to him. I have learned much from his research in Egyptology, some concerning Egypt but more concerning historical methodology. I hope that my own work, including the present book, proves equally stimulating.

    I express my thanks to several individuals for their assistance in the technical production of this volume. Ms. Susan Harvey helped in the editing. Ms. Debbie Estreicher compiled the Index. Ms. Florence Myer typed the manuscript and made excellent suggestions concerning the layout and style. Dr. Charles Bowman of Scholars Press facilitated the production of the book and proved cooperative in all the special problems that constantly occurred.

13 August 1980   Baruch M. Bokser
1 Elul 5740

ABBREVIATIONS

B.	Bavli (Babylonian Talmud)
Ber.	Berakhot
IDB	*Interpreter's Dictionary of the Bible*
JQR	*Jewish Quarterly Review*
M.	Mishnah
T.	Tosefta
Y.	Yerushalmi (Palestinian Talmud)

INTRODUCTION

I

The 1980s promise to be a decade of many rapid changes. Some forecasters suggest that society will undergo transformations that will match those of the industrial revolution. With the prospect of such changes, may we assume that we shall have a new perspective on the past and the present? In particular, what developments may we look forward to in the study of religion, specifically the history of Judaism? Certainly we shall have better means to gather, retrieve, and produce information.[1] But shall we have better or more refined means to assimilate it, to evaluate it, and to determine what is important and significant?

The present volume responds to these questions. It contains seven papers that chart seven different directions that the history of Judaism can take. Each essay treats a critical problem in the study of the ancient, medieval, or modern period and offers a distinct and fresh approach. Each author consciously and explicitly indicates why his task is important and his methodology appropriate. Each one was asked to answer the following specific questions:

1. What are the principal problems or topics on which you work?
2. Why do you deem these problems urgent, in preference to others you might have chosen?
3. What are the chief methods you use to solve the problems on which you work?
4. Why do you find these methods more adequate to the task than others you might have chosen?

The papers respond to the challenge in different ways and reflect the various approaches to the study of Judaism and the intellectual life of Jews. Some of the differences are due to the diverse data and sources under study or the distinctive types of questions posed by the several periods in the history of Judaism. Nevertheless, the papers complement each other, and the procedures described are not limited to the particular period or topic addressed. Scholars in other fields should find the discussions suggestive and should be able to relate them to their own areas of interest. For example, Eisen's questions on the nature and use of sociological and anthropological theory and his and Levine's analysis of the meaning of modernity are also relevant to the premodern eras and to the histories of other religions and groups. Likewise, Neusner's analysis of stories could successfully be applied to medieval and modern Judaism and to other, non-Judaic, literatures. Consequently, the papers are programmatic and provide models of methodologies available to the historian in the 1980s.

II

While the papers reflect different approaches, one can discern in them variations on a single theme. They all deal with the nature, meaning, and impact of change. In our contemporary period, change occurs at a rapid pace while in earlier times, in traditional societies, it occurred much more gradually. Likewise, today new developments and notions are welcomed, while in earlier days they often were feared and ostensibly rejected. But changes did occur. Hence what constitutes a "change" and how can we measure it?[2]

We may exemplify this problem in terms of literary creativity and the development of ideas. In premodern times, people often composed works in an anachronistic manner. Authors drew upon earlier teachings and ideas and presented them in the state of their full development, in the light of the end result--for, it was assumed, was that not its meaning all along? Moreover, ideas frequently lost their individuality and became part of the world view of the group as a whole. How then can we discern the various points of view that preceded the final fruition of the idea or those that were not developed at all in the subsequent generations?

Neusner, Zahavy, Goodblatt, and Ravitzky in different ways address this aspect of the problem.[3] They demonstrate that while we may be able to discern certain developments and find in them significance and universal structures, we can fully appreciate them only if we consider the historical context and the full range of sources, even archaeological ones. These additional materials may throw light on the role of the sources which are normally studied and analyzed. Similarly, can we effectively understand a person's distinctive thought and approach and hence contribution without paying attention to all of his or her intellectual and imaginative expressions? It is for this reason that Blumenthal argues that one must integrate the study of ideas along with experience, philosophy along with mysticism, and treat spirituality as a whole. All of these questions are central to the two papers on modernity. Levine and Eisen challenge conventional pictures of the meaning and impact of modernity on Judaism.

Bokser: Introduction

They do this by criticizing the perspective and the criteria often used to measure change as well as to determine its very existence.

III

Jacob Neusner, in the first paper, "Story as History in Ancient Judaism," provides a justification for the historical enterprise. He discusses what type of history should be written. Aware of a contemporary crisis in education, he formulates this question: Why should a person read history if it only informs one of a fact in the past? Modern culture and science do not need it, for they rely on information that can be gained firsthand. This observation penetrates to the depths of the modern intellectual situation and, as we shall see, is a motif in several of the other papers, in particular in Eisen's treatment of modernity, the last paper.

Neusner suggests that since true history deals with universals and generalities, it properly belongs to general education. Drawing upon the insight of structuralists, he points out that accounts of the past reflect the inner structure of a conflict and resolution to a problem which are potentially applicable to anyone at any time. Hence one must find the inner structures of past events and of their reports. But this is only half of Neusner's thesis. He argues that a true appreciation of a conflict and its resolution must take account of its specificity and accordingly locate it in its historical context. Neusner explains what he means through the analysis of two talmudic narratives. In each a rabbinic figure is contrasted with an alternative type of leadership. In the first we find Ḥoni, a first-century miracle worker, and in the second Vespasian, a foreign political authority. The stories demonstrate that rabbinic leadership, based upon the knowledge of Torah, is greater and more enduring than these other competing forces. Neusner further argues that the analysis must not stop at this point. He asks, since talmudic pericopae often have numerous versions, what accounts for the specific version and what explains the changes? Therefore, in these two cases, why were the stories told at a given time and why were they preserved?

Various literary critics of Midrashim, including Geza Vermes, Joseph Heinemann, and W. S. Towner, have focused upon the variations in stories and have demonstrated how stories are constantly contemporized and revised and, in turn, new elements and notions presented in old garb. Neusner and others have analyzed these two stories and their motifs and have suggested why they are included in rabbinic literature.[4] Likewise, as pointed out by Goodblatt in his paper, recent scholarship has proved that one should not understand rabbinic stories in a literalist fashion. The achievements of these other scholars, though, make us realize the novelty of Neusner's contribution. One must also treat the structuralist message of the narrative. Hence, Neusner's paper provides a paradigm to analyze stories in any period and in any literature. But Neusner transcends the structuralist approach. By arguing that one must locate the universal structure in its historical context, Neusner concludes that the truth gains richness and meaning once one can see how the universal is manifested in a specific time and place. Indeed, we live in a real time and place, and for us to make sense of our own situation, we must learn to recognize universal truths and structures in our own lives.

Neusner thus outlines a twofold program. Analyze a story to find its structure and learn about the historical situation to be able to locate stories in it. The task is urgent. Only in this way will the past be of interest to people other than historians and antiquarians. Only in this way can we effectively deal with the present.

Neusner's essay does not stand in a vacuum and historical analysis of the past has gone through many stages. While critical historians generally no longer try to produce a narrative history,[6] that does not mean they cannot make important contributions. Neusner himself has devoted considerable effort to this endeavor and has made important contributions to the study of Iranian Jewry in Parthian and Sasanian times and to the understanding of the formation of early rabbinic Judaism.[7] He has been especially concerned with placing the legal and aggadic materials within their historical context. It is this second task of elucidating the historical situation that Goodblatt addresses in his paper.

David Goodblatt's "Towards the Rehabilitation of Talmudic History" demonstrates that we may optimistically hope to recover additional reliable information about the historical context of Jewry in late antiquity. It does this by reviewing recent strides in the analysis and use of rabbinic literature, the primary sources for the period. He is aware that writers too often employ sources in an uncritical, even at times literalist, fashion and at times even cite them unsystematically and selectively. When the sources are the talmudic and midrashic literature, the results are worse than in the study of the sources of other periods. Rabbinic literature is highly one-sided, deriving from rabbinic circles and reflecting their world view and self-image. Due to the dearth of other sources, uncritical reliance on these materials will produce a very lopsided picture. Neusner's early work on Iranian Jewry took account of these factors and set the perimeters of what one could know concerning the history of Iranian Jewry. Nevertheless, Goodblatt believes that thanks to a greater sophistication in recent scholarly works and advances in literary studies of the Talmud, further knowledge is now possible. His own book, *Rabbinic Instruction in Sasanian Babylonia*,[8] is one of these important contributions. The implications that we may draw from the findings of the talmudic literary critics provide a source of special confidence. We can now deal with the vexing problem of the dating of specific statements and pericopae. Since we now understand far more about the relationship of the anonymous and attributed materials, we now know to what degree we may rely on attributions. Equipped with these new tools, we can uncover more information; we can be far more exact and hence we are able more reliably to trace changes and developments.[9] Goodblatt's paper thus sets out methodological guidelines to carry out Neusner's second task to locate stories in their historical context, and therefore the two papers complement each other.

Tzvee Zahavy, in "A New Approach to Early Jewish Prayer," takes up a different problem and demonstrates a third approach to the history of Judaism. He claims that research must draw upon the results of several disciplines. But how may one do this without violating the integrity of each?

The topic of Zahavy's essay is rabbinic liturgy. Since prayer constitutes an essential element of any religion, an understanding of its nature should provide insight into a religion's structure, ideas, and rites. His own research treats one set of sources, rabbinic literature, but he realizes there are other sources which may throw light on this topic. In dealing with the complex task of integrating the diverse materials, he asserts that at the outset one must determine what a source represents. Only then, when we know our limitations, can we effectively and fully employ each source. In this vein, Zahavy by way of example examines three bodies of evidence, each in

terms of its own characteristics and function in ancient Jewish
society. The three include: texts of prayers found in rabbinic
literature and post-talmudic standardized prayer books; liturgical rules and regulations in rabbinic literature; and archaeological and material remains from antiquity. Especially notable
are his comments on the indirect information available from the
findings of art historians and archaeologists. They point to the
existence of regional variations among the synagogues and throw
light on synagogue activities and functionaries.[10] Zahavy thus
sees the need for interdisciplinary cooperation. But he argues
that each field must first formulate its own set of questions
appropriate to its data. In this way we shall avoid producing
a homogeneity which will not accord with reality.

The two papers on Judaism in medieval times reflect the
most up-to-date trends and at the same time provide a contrast,
enabling the reader to see two opposite approaches to the study
of medieval Jewish thought and spirituality. Ravitzky, in "Some
Remarks on the Study of Jewish Philosophy in the Middle Ages,"
divides the study of philosophy into primary and secondary
domains. The primary effort is to trace the dynamics of philosophical ideas and their logical developments. To do this--and
herein lies the urgency of his task--one must make use of philosophical works presently found in manuscripts. For fully to
understand a work, even the major philosophical treatises long
known and published in good editions, one must examine not only
the work itself, its predecessors, and possible sources, but also
later works which respond to and develop its ideas. Ravitzky's
method has been applied elsewhere to the analysis of the New
Testament, Gnosticism, Philo, and other areas, including the
legal works of Maimonides.[11] By looking at later developments
and interpretations one becomes sensitive to nuances in an
earlier work, elements that could be extended in several directions. This approach seeks to obviate the difficulty to prove
that a certain earlier notion or movement was the origin of a
later thought, for the earlier notions may have been found only
in embryonic form and could have developed in several different
ways.

Ravitzky's second interest in medieval philosophy
focuses on what he believes is its role in Jewish history. By
this he means the impact it had upon those outside of philosophical circles. He develops his thesis because he believes that
philosophy arises in Judaism when Jews encounter a foreign

culture. The presence of philosophical activity indicates the existence of a confrontation with an alien system. Ravitzky's personal scholarly task again is aided by manuscripts. He has found that manuscripts provide us with examples of philosophical teachings in nonphilosophical works, for example in synagogue sermons. Their use of philosophical ideas reveals the degree to which philosophical controversies permeated the wider Jewish community--and hence the degree to which Jews saw themselves in an encounter with another culture.

Ravitzky's comments apparently follow one of the two basic explanations for the rise of Jewish philosophy. According to the first one, philosophy arises in response to external stimuli. The alternative theory argues that internal developments play a significant role as well, and philosophers saw their task not just as a defensive one but as a positive activity too, as the fulfillment of a religious requirement.[12] Certainly this controversy depends in part upon disparate evaluations of the subtle ways in which people participate in a wider culture and assimilate values and notions around them. Such arguments abound throughout the study of the history of Judaism and other cultures. An analogous argument concerns the nature and impact of Hellenism upon Judaism: To what degree was Judaism in the Second Temple period "Hellenized."[13]

Ravitzky's contribution to this controversy, though, provides interesting insights. Ironically, however, since Ravitzky is primarily concerned with the internal development of philosophical ideas, he can go forward with his studies irrespective of the question of outside influence or stimuli. It is clear that with his diachronic approach he will uncover significant historical data and we may look forward to new chapters in the history of philosophy.

The impressiveness of Ravitzky's agendum underscores what David Blumenthal might call its limitations. In his paper, "On Studying Philosophical Mysticism," Blumenthal claims that the traditional effort at tracing the history of philosophical ideas is hampered methodologically. Philosophers lived in a wider context than just that of philosophical ideas. When we speak of Judaism in medieval times, it is arbitrary and fallacious to distinguish between philosophy and other religious and intellectual trends, including mysticism.

Blumenthal does not discuss the significance of intellectual, religious, or spiritual activity in terms of its "impact"

upon large numbers of Jews. Granted, Blumenthal alludes to
Goitein's thesis that Jews under Medieval Islam followed a popular rationalism;[14] nevertheless he does not justify his task on
the basis of the size of the audience. Rather he finds justification in being better able to understand the world view of
central Jewish thinkers in medieval times. Hence one--or, at
least, he--must tackle a problem which is propodeutic to the
study of the history of any particular philosophical idea or controversy. He argues that one must analyze the thought and mind
of Jews in an integrated manner, in particular under the rubric
of "philosophical mysticism." His thesis rests upon the claim
that those traditionally labelled as "mystics" often dealt with
the same problems with which "philosophers" grappled. Moreover,
Blumenthal in a way somewhat similar to Ravitzky's search for
embryonic antecedents stresses that philosophers often served as
sources of inspiration for later mystics, and hence their philosophical works must contain mystical elements, if only in
potential form.

Blumenthal's position is controversial and he has presented parts of it in a fuller form elsewhere.[15] While various
scholars have undertaken important research from this perspective, and Blumenthal does refer to their publications,[16] some
students of philosophy and of mysticism have been hesitant to
accept it. Once Blumenthal finishes the work which he outlines
here, his evidence should provide a decisive argument. But at
this point we are indebted to him for the questions he raises.
He forcefully sensitizes us to the fact that many historians are
guided by faulty assumptions which determine what they consider
worthwhile to study and what questions they deem relevant to ask.
Blumenthal challenges us to take seriously the wider context of
a religious thinker, to investigate all aspects of that person's
interests and personality. Only then can we hope to understand
the full dimension of a writer. While Blumenthal is aware of
the importance of the historical background, he believes the
essential task is to understand the thinker's world view.
Accordingly, one must first examine the thinker's synthesis
which he has formed out of the various parts of his thought.
In a sense, Blumenthal's approach is reminiscent of "new criticism" in literature. The sources of a writer are less important
than their combination and the new unity which they make up.

We may make a final observation concerning Ravitzky's and
Blumenthal's divergent approaches. The differences may reflect

wider differences and an ancient and recurring debate concerning what motivates and characterizes an individual. Do ideas have their own autonomy or does an individual's mental and psychological processing of the ideas determine his or her thought? Certainly the present instance of this long-standing controversy has its own nuances and it may throw light on similar controversies in the study of other forms of spirituality and thought. But we cannot pretend to solve this problem. As a historian, however, I can point out that people do differ. Some are driven by "ideas" and others by the psychological and mental dimensions of their personalities. Moreover, individuals can go through different periods and moods. The 1980 Picasso exhibit in the Museum of Modern Art, New York City, demonstrates how many different approaches and understandings of reality can be experienced by a single person.

Levine's and Eisen's papers deal with Judaism in modern times and take different approaches concerning the means to evaluate the impact of modernity on Judaism. They both suggest that current scholarship has not treated the problem with sufficient subtlety.

Levine deals with the early modern period, eighteenth-century Poland. He believes this area and time period deserve his attention since then major transformations occurred in Europe and the events in Poland in particular had a great effect on later Jewry. Because this impact extends to the twentieth century, especially in America, his project can throw light on the contemporary scene. Nevertheless, his paper does confront a central historiographic problem: What constitutes a "response" to a challenge or competing system?

Levine argues that adapting to the modern situation does not necessarily only involve adopting the "modern values." Rather it encompasses whatever one does in response to the new "modern" situation, including rejecting it. Hence one must avoid imposing one's own values and one model of a response, in this case that of Western Europe, on the choices that people made. Jews--or any individuals or group--may evaluate a new trend and decide that their best alternative is to reject it and its values.

In applying his thesis to Polish Jewry, Levine rejects Weber's claim that Jewish other-worldliness involved an obliviousness to the surrounding world due to "Talmudic scholasticism or Jewish punctiliousness in the observance of ritual or the need of Jews to control their overflowing and dangerous '*ressentement*.'"[17] Rather it formed part of a conscious reaction to the failure of Polish nationalism and worldly political action. Likewise, Jews generally exhibited little interest in science not out of ignorance but as a response based upon the Jewish situation.

In suggesting that we be more receptive and more open to the complexities and diversity of responses, including antimodernists and moderate modernists as well as modernists, Levine is in accord with various scholars who deal with the modern and earlier periods.[18] Recent events provide numerous examples of Jews and others who have questioned many of the "modern" notions and their supposed benefits. Whatever the benefits or harm to psychological and mental health of such a response, we should not believe that it is made in ignorance.[19]

Levine thus provides us with another example of the variations and complexities in human responses. The more we know of the wider context, in this case Polish history and the general European situation, the better we are able to appreciate the significance of the Jewish posture. Moreover, we may be able to uncover significant changes and transformations in the midst of what appears to be traditional activity.

Since Levine connects the social context with the religious and intellectual developments, it would be of interest to trace what happens to the particular Judaic response once the reasons for the reaction pass and Jews live in a new context. To what degree do the patterns gain a certain degree of autonomy? In addition, to what degree does the Jewish heritage provide a predilection that may affect the choice of response to the social situation? Considering Levine bases his interest in Polish Jewry on its significance for later Judaism, we can look forward to his extending his investigation to the post-eighteenth-century period.

Arnold Eisen in the past paper, "The Uses of Social Theory in the Study of Modern Judaism," depicts the struggles of a researcher in employing modern sociological and anthropological theories in the study of modern Judaism. Eisen delineates two overall problems. First, the theories are developed on the basis of one set of data, often that of a majority religion and culture, Protestantism, and applied to a different set of data, that of a minority, Judaism. Second, the theorists may have been guided by certain assumptions or "faith commitments"

and hence their work is too biased. Eisen further indicates that
the theories may entail divergent orientations and cannot be
simply integrated or eclectically drawn upon. Yet to provide
meaning to the specific materials under study and to transcend
the details--as Neusner also argued in his paper--one must employ
theories.

Eisen perceives an urgency in his task because he believes
that modern Jewish thinkers have not adequately dealt with the
challenge of modernity. He draws upon the theorists to determine
what he believes to be the significant issues. Most Jewish
thinkers have dealt with perennial Jewish problems. Yet the
modern situation differs from premodern times in three significant ways. These are changes in the perception of, first, the
mind, as exemplified in the work of Freud; second, of an individual's relation to history and the past; and third, of the
world order as a result of modern science. Whenever modern
thinkers have treated these topics, they are superficial and on
the defensive, and do not probe the nature of the modern situation. He believes people and Jews in modern times reject the
claims of the past. They do not automatically believe they
should live up to a past definition of a "Jew." Rather they
seek to forge their own identity. He plans to investigate the
impact of this change on Judaism and Jewish institutions. At
the completion of his research we can evaluate the degree to
which this modern "self-consciousness" actually poses a problem
to the majority of Jews and to contemporary expressions of
Judaism. But at this point, Eisen's essay serves to emphasize
that theories which we employ do not originate in a vacuum and
that people differ concerning not only the questions and problems that should be examined but also the selection of data and
the whole direction of the inquiry.

IV

The seven papers thus carefully treat specific topics
yet also provide programmatic statements. They indicate that
the discipline of history is not dead. It can sustain and
inspire minds to continue to delve into the past, to uncover the
background to our contemporary situation, and thereby to understand ourselves better--and it can do this in a refreshing and
stimulating manner. With the prospect of impending swift and
significant changes in our society in the 1980s, we shall need
an even better sense of orientation and perspective on the past.

Consequently, our task is to select our subject and methodologies appropriate to it and to pursue our chosen area of research.
In the future we can evaluate how the programs presented here actually bore fruit and provided new insight to study the history of Judaism.

NOTES TO INTRODUCTION

[1] As one colleague put it, the 1970s was the decade of photocopying and xeroxing, and the 1980s will be that of the computer. Thus in late 1979 there appeared the first volume of the long-awaited *Concordance to the Talmud Yerushalmi (Palestinian Talmud)*, by Moshe Kosovsky (Jerusalem, 1979). This work was compiled in part by a computerized system.

[2] For a definition of "traditional" society see Jacob Katz, *Tradition and Crisis* (New York, 1971) and *Out of the Ghetto* (New York, 1978). The issue is not whether change occurred but rather how it was perceived. Every creative intellectual and artistic endeavor produced something new. But traditionalists generally believed that their understanding of religious texts and ideas merely uncovered something that was there already. This phenomenon may help explain the fact that frequently one religious source may rewrite and revise an earlier one and thereby incorporate a later interpretation of the earlier source directly into the text. This is found in the "rewritten Midrash" genre and throughout rabbinic legal and aggadic works. A midrashic pericope is constantly contemporized and a talmudic baraita recomposed. See below, n. 4, and the text thereto, and Baruch M. Bokser, *Post Mishnaic Judaism in Transition: Samuel on Berakhot and the Beginnings of Gemara* (Chicago, 1980), pp. 429-42 and nn. for a full discussion and bibliography. Isadore Twersky has described how the halakhist's desire to uncover the meaning of God's message had both conservative and innovative implications, to justify and to limit personal creativity. See Isadore Twersky, *Rabad of Posquieres*, rev. ed. (Philadelphia, 1980), pp. xix-xxv. Avi Ravitsky, below pp. 79-80, n. 11, points to the conservative perception among medieval philosophers. Therefore, it is not surprising that those advocating adoption of "modern" notions chose to describe their innovations in traditional terms. See Hillel Levine, "'Dwarfs on the Shoulders of Giants'; A Case Study in the Impact of Modernization on the Social Epistemology of Judaism," *Jewish Social Studies* 40 (1978):63-72.

[3] William Scott Green in his paper, "Reading and The Writing of Rabbinism: Toward an Interpretation of Rabbinic Literature," also addressed this problem. As indicated in the Preface, this paper will appear elsewhere. Meanwhile see his earlier paper, "What's in a Name--The Problematic of Rabbinic 'Biography,'" in *Approaches to Ancient Judaism: Theory and Practice* (Missoula, Mont., 1978), pp. 77-96.

[4] See, e.g., Jacob Neusner, *Development of a Legend: Studies on the Traditions Concerning Yohanan ben Zakkai* (Leiden, 1970); Anthony J. Saldarini, "Johanan Ben Zakkai's Escape from Jerusalem: Origin and Development of a Rabbinic Story," *Journal for the Study of Judaism in the Persian, Hellenistic, and Roman Period* 6 (1975):189-204; and W. S. Green, "Palestinian Holy Men: Charismatic Leadership and Rabbinic Tradition," in *Aufstieg und Niedergang der Römischen Welt*. II, 19.2 (Berlin, 1979), pp. 619-47. See also Geza Vermes, *Scripture and Tradition in Judaism* (Leiden, 1973); Joseph Heinemann, *Aggadah and Its Development* (Jerusalem, 1974); and W. S. Towner, *The Rabbinic "Enumeration of Scriptural Examples"* (Leiden, 1973).

[5] See below, p. 35 and n. 5.

[6] See e.g., C. Van Woodward, review of *The Civil War: A Narrative*, Vol. 3: *Red River to Appomattox* by Shelby Foote, *New York Review of Books*, March 6, 1975, p. 12.

[7] Jacob Neusner, *A History of the Jews in Babylonia* 1, 2d ed. (Leiden, 1969), 2-5 (Leiden, 1966-1970). His works on early rabbinic Judaism include *The Rabbinic Traditions About the Pharisees Before 70*, 3 vols. (Leiden, 1971), *Eliezer ben Hyrcanus: The Tradition and the Man*, 2 vols. (Leiden, 1973), and the studies on the history of mishnaic law, cited below, p. 59, n. 18.

Literary analysis and observation often can produce interesting results which have significant historical implications. See e.g., Neusner's observations, below pp. 25 and 29, n. 15; Abraham Joshua Heschel, *A Passion for Truth* (New York, 1973), p. 70; and Baruch M. Bokser, "Redaction Criticism of the Talmud: The Case of Ḥanina Ben Dosa" (forthcoming).

[8] David Goodblatt, *Rabbinic Instruction in Sasanian Babylonia* (Leiden, 1975).

[9] See Goodblatt's nn., in particular his critical review of the literature in *Aufstieg und Niedergang der Römischen Welt*, to which add Bokser, *Post Mishnaic Judaism*.

[10] Zahavy himself points out that research must investigate additional areas, including the prerabbinic history of the liturgy. By this he would mean the type of studies undertaken by Shemaryahu Talmon, "The Emergence of Institutionalized Prayer in Israel in the Light of the Qumrân Literature," in *Qumrân. Sa piété, sa théologie et son milieu*, ed. M. Delcor [= *Bibliotheca Ephemeridum Theologicarum Lovaniensium* 46 (1978)] (Lovain, 1978), pp. 265-84; and N. M. Sarna, "The Psalm Superscriptions and the Guilds," in *Studies in Jewish Religious and Intellectual History Presented to Alexander Altmann*, ed. Siegfried Stein and Raphael Loewe (University, Ala., 1980), pp. 281-300.

[11] See for example, Birger A. Pearson, *Philo and the Gnostics on Man and Salvation*. The Center for Hermeneutical Studies in Hellenistic and Modern Culture. *Protocol of the Twenty-Ninth Colloquy: 17 April 1977*, ed. W. Wuellner; and Isadore Twersky, *Introduction to the Code of Maimonides (Mishneh Torah)* (New Haven, 1980), p. 55.

[12] See e.g., Herbert A. Davidson, "The Study of Philosophy as a Religious Obligation," in *Religion in a Religious Age*, ed. S. D. Goitein (Cambridge, 1974), pp. 53-68; and Jacob Neusner, *The Way of Torah*, 3d ed. (North Scituate, Mass., 1979), pp. 73-75.

[13] See e.g., Elias Bickerman, *From Ezra to the Last Days of the Maccabees* (New York, 1962); H. L. Ginzberg, *Kohelet: A New Commentary* (Tel Aviv, 1961), pp. 51-52; Martin Hengel, *Judaism and Hellenism*, English 2d rev. and enl. ed., 2 vols. (Philadelphia, 1974); Jacob Neusner, *Early Rabbinic Judaism* (Leiden, 1975), pp. 139-215; Morton Smith, "The Image of God: Notes on the Hellenization of Judaism, with Especial Reference to Goodenough's Work on Jewish Symbols," *Bulletin of the John Rylands Library* 40 (1958):473-512, and *Palestinian Parties and Politics that Shaped the Old Testament* (New York, 1971); and Victor Tcherikover, *Hellenistic Civilization and the Jews* (Philadelphia, 1959).

[14] See e.g., S. D. Goitein, "Religion in Everyday Life as Reflected in the Documents of the Cairo Geniza," in his *Religion in a Religious Age*.

[15] David Blumenthal, "Maimonides' Intellectualist Mysticism and the Superiority of the Prophecy of Moses," *Studies in Medieval Culture* 10 (1977):51-67.

[16] See below p. 84. Cf. Hamid Algar, "The Study of Islam: The Work of Henry Corbin," *Religious Studies Review* 6 (1980):85-91, concerning the study of Islamic spirituality.

[17] Quoted from Levine, below p. 115.

[18] See e.g., Katz, *Out of the Ghetto*; Katz, "Contributions Towards a Biography of R. Moses Sofer," in *Studies in Mysticism and Religion Presented to Gershom G. Scholem*, ed. E. E. Urbach et al. (Jerusalem, 1967), Hebrew pp. 115-48; Jacob Neusner, *Between Time and Eternity* (Encino, Calif., 1975), pp. 124-26.
Various critical scholarly concerns associated with Western Europe may find roots or earlier analogues in the East. See Chaim Zalman Dimitrovsky, "One Hundred Fifty Years of Rabbinic Scholarship," paper read at the 42nd annual meeting of the American Academy for Jewish Research, December 28, 1969. See also n. 13 and text thereto.

[19] See e.g., Charles S. Liebman, "Orthodox Judaism Today," *Midstream* 25, no. 7 (August-September, 1979):19-26. He describes how one modern traditionalist group, modern orthodox Jews, compartmentalize their lives; they live certain aspects of modernity yet reject its intellectual ideology.

PART ONE

JUDAISM IN ANCIENT TIMES

CHAPTER ONE

STORY AS HISTORY IN ANCIENT JUDAISM
Formulating Fresh Questions

Jacob Neusner
Brown University

Studies in the history of Judaism over the next ten years will not only ask new questions, as other papers in this volume have shown. They will also address familiar texts. For the materials of Judaism, particularly in ancient times, are, in general, well known. In this paper I propose to frame a set of questions to be addressed to Talmudic stories about holy men of Judaism and the things they did and said. Since the context of discourse is the history of Judaism, a subdivision of the history of religions, the framing of these questions must at the outset find its location in the larger setting of hermeneutical issues confronting the history of religions. Finally, since the history of religions itself forms a subdivision of that part of general education organized within the humanities, to begin with the entire enterprise must be founded upon issues of general educational, humanistic interest. These are the considerations which account for the close attention paid to context at the outset of this paper, which is meant to provide both a program for a decade (or more) of work and the illustration and exemplification of the stated program in religions-historical interpretation.

I

THE CONTEXT

All learning should aim to contribute to general education. By general education I mean not common literacy in an established canon of writings, but insight accessible to people without regard to prior traits of culture, race, sex, class, or nation. I cannot raise a topic in the study of Judaism, therefore, without proposing to address issues of general intelligibility. These are issues of general education, the humanities, and religious studies. Even though the framing of an appropriate address for discourse is brief, it is critical in establishing context and preparing the way for questions of method and meaning.

What I mean by general education is explained by Jonathan Z. Smith, who defines it as the "notion of providing *exempli gratia*, an arsenal of classic instances which are held to be exemplary, of providing paradigmatic events and expressions as resources from which to reason, from which to extend the possibility of intelligibility to that which first appears to be novel."[1] From Smith, also, comes a striking and pertinent definition of the "humanities," which, at its origins, in fifteenth-century Italian humanism, was a word set in contrast with its opposite. "Humane studies" were to be contrasted with "divine sciences," the humanities with theology.

Now in that context, the study of religion could not be part of the humanities. Matters changed so that religion became a topic of generally accessible discourse only when the distinction was made between two parallel paths in the study of religion, a humanistic one for the academy, a theological one for the seminary.[2] So there are these two matters. First is the interest in general education, that is, in showing how one small matter exemplifies some larger concern of broad interest and accessibility. Second, there is the determination of finding a humanistic program for the study of religions. Combining the two is not difficult. What we have to do is precede each specific statement with a general one, and place an *e.g.* between the two. That is, we should seek for what is general in what is particular, showing how the facts of a given culture, race, sex, class, nation, or religion, in particular, illuminate the condition of culture, race, sex, class, nation, religion, in general. In the case of the study of religion, we have to take seriously the heritage of the Enlightenment, which sees religion as a generic, distinct from the collectivity of specific, believing communities. The Enlightenment, moreover, maintains that any human fact lies within the range of reason and is susceptible to shared understanding. So, carrying Smith's excellent program forward, I wish to offer, as an exercise in exemplification, a problem in the analysis of ancient Judaism in its principal expression, that is, the Judaism of the Mishnah, Talmud, and midrashic compilations of the first six centures of the Common Era. This I wish to do in such a way that I may contribute to general education in the context of the humanistic study of religion.

II

THE PROBLEM

The issue to be exemplified in the study of ancient Jewish texts is nothing less than our basic judgment upon the past and its relevance, that is, upon history and how it should be studied. What I wish to do is to show how we may discover questions appropriate to historical facts in our hands. I present an exercise in exemplifying the discovery of correct questions to be addressed to ancient sources. Stories drawn out of ancient Judaism will serve as our laboratory case, so Judaism will provide a paradigm of interpretation, a resource from which to reason. To state matters rapidly and superficially, modern culture rejects the claims of history. The scholarly aspect of culture—that is, culture as nurtured in universities—today works itself out essentially independent of the past and, it must follow, independent, too, of the material and social reality of the present. That is why architecture, music, philosophy, literature and the reading of texts work out their programs of study without regard to the history of architecture, music, philosophy, literature, let alone the history of the study of these subjects. As Carl Schorske states, "The modern mind has been growing indifferent to history because history, conceived as a continuous nourishing tradition, has become useless to it."[3] Evidence for this fact is drawn by Schorske from developments in diverse fields of learning. New critics in literature, he points out, replace literary historicism with "an a-temporal, internalistic, formal analysis." Traditional political philosophy gives way to "the a-historical and politically neutralizing reign of the behaviorists." In philosophy, as Schorske says, "a discipline previously marked by a high consciousness of its own historical character and continuity, the analytic school challenged the validity of the traditional questions that had concerned philosophers since antiquity. In the interest of a restricted and purer functioning in the areas of language and logic, the new philosophy broke the ties both to history . . . and to the discipline's own past."

What is important is that the new methods of analysis in the humanistic fields, which stressed internal traits and autonomous, enduring characteristics of structure and style, made the break from history. That is, once it is recognized that creations of literature and art adhere to canons of logic unbound by context but expressive of a universal and timeless "logic," whether of language or of morphology, then history as the story of where things come from and what they mean because of where they come from no longer explains very much. And, as Schorske says, "the historian could ignore [these autonomous characteristics of structure and style] only at the risk of misreading the historical meaning of his material." Let me now cite Schorske's fine statement of the problem, before turning to the exemplification of the problem in the study of stories told by ancient rabbis in the Talmud. This extended statement constitutes that generalization, to which the study of Judaism supplies its "e.g.":

> . . . The historian will not share to the full the aim of the humanistic textual analyst. The latter aims at the greatest possible illumination of a cultural product, relativizing all principles of analysis to its particular content. The historian seeks rather to locate and interpret the artifact temporally in a field where two lines intersect. One line is vertical, or diachronic, by which he establishes the relation of a text or a system of thought to previous expressions in the same branch of cultural activity. . . . The other is horizontal or synchronic; by it [the historian] assesses the relation of the content of the intellectual object to what is appearing in other branches or aspects of a culture at the same time. . . .[4]

Let me now restate the problem as I wish to confront it. For a long time, from the beginning of the nineteenth century, history was deemed to provide the principal road into the interpretation of artifacts of culture, whether literary or philosophical or political or religious. The means of description and of explanation were one and the same: this is what happened, so this is what it meant. Consequently, when confronted with the need to describe a religion, people took for granted the issue was an essentially historical one. Explanation followed from the mode of description. The facts adduced in a given order and by a given program carry with them the explanation induced by that order and demanded by that program. Explanation and interpretation then became subdivisions of history, and meaning emerged from explanation. So what happened in the past was deemed to bear within itself its own claim upon the present. Theories of society emerged from histories of society, and so in the other fields of learning. Since, in the nature of things, learning shapes culture, and culture governs society and its material reality, it would follow that what had happened imparted meaning upon what was happening. History became doctrine, "historicism" viewed from the perspective of values.

Attacks on an essentially historical, hence traditional, view of culture seemed to come only from barbarians like Henry

Ford, who said, "History is bunk." The citadel of historicism would not fall before mechanics. The point at which the historical reading and explanation of the artifacts of culture proved vulnerable lay outside of the citadel entirely. The great theories never collapse; people simply walk away from them. In the case of historicism, moreover, we deal with a variety of specific versions of the matter, consequently with a sequence of settings in which an other-than-historicistic theory of explanation and interpretation would replace the established one. In one setting, it would be a philosophical attack. In another, the discovery of enduring structures of mind, beyond time and circumstance, would call into question the developmental and orderly description which then passed for interpretation. In still a third, the logic embodied in the genetic fallacy would be overturned, so that origins no longer were found adequately to explain even themselves. In a fourth, the end of the fallacy that beginnings explain all carried in its wake the collapse of the notion that historical description contains any explanation at all. And so it would go. In the end matters were as Schorske sets them forth: history seemed bankrupt, to everyone but historians.

The issue is now to be drawn more concretely. To ask the question as simply as I can: How shall we read a story or a text? What do we think is important about that story? So at the outset the matter of history as against ahistory concerns the very purpose of learning, the context of interpretation. Once we determine that our interests are other-than-historical, in the sense of history as the story of one-time events, as narrative, it is obvious that we shall interpret texts from an other-than-historical perspective. We shall want to know different things, so we shall observe different traits. The challenge to a historical reading of stories and texts comes from a simple fact. Historians do not deem important, or even notice, traits of literary structure which call into question whether stories are meant to contain history at all. There are structural traits pointing to the original meaning and purpose of making up and telling a story. These in their nature simply preclude the pertinence of simple analysis of historical, including philological, traits. History and philology are interesting but not urgent. The reason is that to ancient fables and tales, including those of a historical character, they present the wrong questions. So their results prove beside the point. That is one position of that structuralism to which Schorske alludes.

In what follows, I shall lead you through three positions: examples of (1) a historicistic reading of two Jewish tales of ancient times, (2) a structuralist reading on these same stories, and then, at the end, (3) a post-structuralist reversion to questions of a fundamentally historical character. But these are different ones from those asked at the outset. From asking what really happened "behind" a story (the kernel of truth), I shall move to questions of what is happening in a given social setting through the principal didactic message of a story. For before us is obviously not an account of one-time events, history in the old sense. Rather, revealed are persistent traits of social culture and of mind, history in a mode congruent to the character and purposes of the evidence. That is the structure of this paper.

III

THE PROBLEM EXEMPLIFIED IN ANCIENT JUDAISM

Story and History

These rather general remarks demand concrete and specific exemplification. For that purpose, I wish to take up two stories found in ancient rabbinic writings and to show how they have been used for historical purposes. By attending to the structural traits of these stories, I then shall show that the use of such stories for history misinterprets the obvious purposes of the tellers of those stories. This I shall do by demonstrating on the basis of the structural traits of those stories just what the storytellers wished to accomplish. In this way we shall see why historicism misreads the historical meaning of these materials. The reason is that asking what really happened, or assuming that what the story says happened really did happen, misses the point of the story. The original and generative purpose of telling the story is on the surface, accessible to us because it is revealed by the basic structure of the story, its emphases, organization, points of conflict and the resolution of conflict. Stories are not history in so simple a sense as is assumed by a narrowly historical reading of stories. The reason is that they do not contain evidence of one-time events but speak of enduring social truths—a different sort of history.

Let us first of all take up the two stories, then rapidly draw upon a part of the record of what has been said about and done with them by people to whom historical description, interpretation, and explanation constitute a single and simultaneous act: historians in search of a narrative of events. The first story deals with a miracle-worker and what he did ("one time"); the second, with a rabbi and what he did ("on that day"). These are two distinct types of historical person in the rabbinic literature, the former, as the name states, capable of affecting nature, the latter the principal heroic type of the rabbinic kind of Judaism. At the outset let us simply see the stories as they appear, in English translation, in their original settings.

The first hero is Ḥoni, the circle-drawer, and how he made rain.

> A. They said to Ḥoni, the circle-drawer, "Pray for rain."
>
> He said to them, "Go and take in the clay ovens used for Passover, so that they do not soften [in the rain that is coming]." He prayed, but it did not rain.
>
> What did he do? He drew a circle and stood in the middle of it and said before Him, "Lord of the world! Your children have turned to me, for before You, I am like a member of the family. I swear by Your great name--I'm simply not moving from here until you take pity on your children!" It began to rain drop by drop.
>
> B. He said, "This is not what I wanted, but rain for filling up cisterns, pits, and caverns." It began to rain violently.
>
> C. He said, "This is not what I wanted, but rain of good will, blessing, and graciousness." Now it rained the right way, until Israelites had to flee from Jerusalem up to the Temple Mount because of the rain.
>
> D. Now they came and said to him, "Just as you prayed for it to rain, now pray for it to go away." He said to them, "Go, see whether the stone of the strayers is disappeared."
>
> E. Simeon b. Shataḥ sent [a message] to him, "If you were not Ḥoni, I should decree a ban of excommunication against you. But what am I going to do to you? For you make demands before the Omnipresent so he does what you want, like a son who makes demands on his father so he does what he wants. Concerning you Scripture says, *Let your father and your mother be glad, and let her that bore you rejoice* (Prov. 23:25)."[5]

For the present, it suffices to note that the principal action of the story is in a sequence of three events (B, C, D), rain drop by drop, violent rain, and the right kind of rain—but for too long. The story trails off, and Ḥoni ceases to be the chief actor, at D. The message of Simeon, E, is totally without preparation. It appears to be tacked on, and the saying stands outside of the narrative materials, to which it does not make reference.

Let us now turn to the second story, which is of a more obviously historical character. This story deals with the

destruction of the Temple in Jerusalem in A.D. 70 and establishes
a link of continuity between that Temple and a schoolhouse of
Judaism located in Yavneh (Jamnia), a town just off the southern
coast of the Land of Israel. The second hero is Yoḥanan ben
Zakkai, who (as this story tells us) is the one who effected the
movement from the doomed Temple to the nascent schoolhouse, from
cult to learning, from priest to rabbi, and from independent
state to subordinated, autonomous holy nation. (But this view of
the focus of the story is wrong, as I shall suggest in a moment.)

A. When Vespasian came to destroy Jerusalem, he said
to the inhabitants, "Fools, why do you seek to destroy this
city, and why do you seek to burn the Temple? For what do
I ask of you but that you send me one bow or one arrow, and
I shall leave you?" They said to him, "Even as we went
forth against the first two who were here before thee and
slew them, so shall we go forth against thee and slay thee."

B. When Rabban Yoḥanan ben Zakkai heard this, he sent
for the men of Jerusalem and said to them, "My children,
why do you destroy this city, and why do you seek to burn
the Temple? For what is it that he asks of you? He asks
of you one bow or one arrow, and he will go off from you."
They said to him, "Even as we went forth against the two
before him and slew them, so shall we go forth against him
and slay him."

C. Vespasian had men stationed near the walls of Jerusalem. Every word which they overheard they would write
down, attach [the message] to an arrow and shoot it over
the wall, saying that Rabban Yoḥanan ben Zakkai was one
of the Emperor's supporters. Now, after Rabban Yoḥanan
ben Zakkai had spoken to them one day, two days and three
days, and they still would not listen to him, he sent for
his disciples, for Rabbi Eliezer and Rabbi Joshua. "My
sons," he said to them, "arise and take me out of here.
Make a coffin for me that I might lie in it." Rabbi
Eliezer took the head end of it, Rabbi Joshua took hold
of the foot; and they began carrying him as the sun set,
until they reached the gates of Jerusalem. "Who is this?"
the gatekeepers demanded. "It's a dead man," they replied.
"Do you not know that the dead may not be held overnight
in Jerusalem?" "If it's a dead man," the gatekeepers said
to them, "take him out." They continued carrying him until
they reached Vespasian.

D. They opened the coffin, and [Rabban Yoḥanan ben
Zakkai] stood up before him. "Are you Rabban Yoḥanan ben
Zakkai?" [Vespasian] inquired; "Tell me, what may I give
you?" "I ask of you only Yavneh, where I might go and
teach my disciples and there establish a prayer [house]
and perform all the commandments." "Go," Vespasian said
to him, "and whatever you wish to do, do."

E. Said [Rabban Yoḥanan] to him, "By your leave, may
I say something to you?" "Speak," [Vespasian] said to
him. Said [Rabban Yoḥanan] to him, "Lo, you [already]
stand as royalty." "How do you know this?" [Vespasian
asked]. [Rabban Yoḥanan] replied, "This has been handed
down to us, that the Temple will not be surrendered to a
commoner, but to a king; as it is said, 'And he shall

cut down the thickets of the forest with iron, and Lebanon shall fall by a mighty one' (Is. 10:34)." It was said: no more than a day, or two or three days, passed before a pair of men reached him from his city [announcing] that the emperor was dead and that he had been elected to succeed as king.[6]

    This story is in five parts, two before the escape from Jerusalem, the escape itself, then two parts after the escape. The focus of interest in the protagonists runs from Vespasian to Yoḥanan, then, at the other end, from Yoḥanan and what he wants to Vespasian and what he wants. We shall not be detained by the problem of chronology or by trying to correlate the tale with the chronicle of Josephus concerning the war against Rome.[7] To do so would foreclose discussion of what is important about this story, that is, what question to begin with is to come to bear upon it.

IV

BEYOND HISTORICISM

    The two tales before us have performed long and honorable service for historians. Both of them pop up in all historical accounts of the history of the Jewish people in the Land of Israel. Ḥoni appears as a miracle-worker. Yoḥanan ben Zakkai figures in every account of the destruction of the Temple. So the events depicted are things that really happened, at the time at which the storyteller says they happened, to real people. These report one-time events. The sayings attributed to the participants in the story really were said, by the people to whom they are assigned, at some one time, and for some one purpose. History is particular. It tells not about the on-going struggles and values of a social group. It reveals not enduring traits of culture. Reality is specific, and, as I said, it happens once for all time. True, a certain skepticism about obvious miracles will figure. It is conventional to avoid total gullibility about Honi's power. But that skepticism serves a limited purpose. Concerning the story about Yoḥanan and Vespasian there are no reservations whatsoever. When we have accomplished the proper exegesis of the story, with stress on philology, lo and behold, we have history. So the methodology of history governs the interpretation of these stories. In this context it is appropriate to cite the wise observation of William Dever, "'Methodology' in archaeology, as in any theory of human inquiry, grows directly out of theory: how you look at the evidence depends on what you want to know and why you think it may be important."[8]

Now let me briefly substantiate this statement of how the two stories have been used. First, the story about Ḥoni has routinely served to prove the character of Jewish magical praxis in the time in which Ḥoni is supposed to have lived, three hundred years before the redaction of the Mishnah, in which the story first appears and is preserved. To take one among innumerable examples, Joshua Trachtenberg writes, "One of the most picturesque of ancient Jewish miracle-workers was Ḥoni HaMeʿagel (first century B.C.E.), whose penchant for standing within a circle while he called down rain from heaven won him his title, 'the circle-drawer.'"[9] In this sentence we see that the story is deemed fact, historical fact, about a one-time event and a person who lived in a particular place. The article on Ḥoni in the *Encyclopaedia Judaica*[10] begins, "Renowned miracle worker in the period of the Second Temple. . . . The Talmud recounts wondrous tales as to the manner in which his prayers for rain were answered." So far as I know, these "tales" in fact add up to the *one* which we considered. To be sure, the story occurs in diverse compilations, from the Mishnah onward. So I suppose we are expected to count each time the story is told as evidence of yet another miracle of rain-making. Later in the same article, the author states, "Ḥoni appears as a charismatic personality and the people considered him undoubtedly a kind of folk prophet with the ability to work miracles. Even Simeon b. Shetaḥ, despite his displeasure with Ḥoni's self-confidence and his wish to place Ḥoni under a ban, was compelled to give way to those who regarded Ḥoni as a 'son who importunes his father.'" To be sure, this paraphrase reads into the tale more than is there. But what is important in this routine account is the frame of reference. It is entirely historical. The story *is* history: a one-time event, a particular person. Ḥoni is not made to typify or to express an established ideal, value, or philosophy. He does not serve as an expression of social conflict or class phenomenon. He is a person. He lived at a given time (first century B.C.E.). He did certain things. He is important because we know who he was and what he did.

The story about Yoḥanan ben Zakkai's emergence from the dying city of Jerusalem, through a coffin, to a new mode of life in Judaism, invariably yields a history of a concrete event. Let me cite one important instance of how the story is utilized:

> It is the accepted view among scholars regarding the negotiations between Vespasian . . . and Rabban Joḥanan b. Zakkai that the latter, when he foresaw the destruction of Jerusalem and the burning of the Temple, sought

to take preventive measures to avert the collapse of the nation and its Torah by establishing a 'spiritual center,' which would assure the continued existence of the Jewish people, even when its residual political independence was gone and its homeland destroyed. . . .[11]

Gedalyahu Alon, who wrote these words, goes on to address this question to the story we read (and some of its parallels): "What prompted Rabban Joḥanan to go particularly to Jabneh?" The reason the question is to be asked is that Alon assumes the story can answer it. The story takes for granted there was some reason to go to that place, and Alon takes for granted the story tells us what really happened. As it happens, Alon takes Yavneh to be a kind of concentration point for Jews who had surrendered to the Romans or were friendly to begin with: "[They] went to Jabneh not because they particularly desired this place, but because they were sent against their will . . . Rabban Joḥanan's main request to Vespasian that he should be allowed 'to study Torah [at Jabneh] and make fringes and perform there all the other precepts' simply means that their captors should not make the conditions of their confinement unduly stringent, as they were, apparently, wont to do with others. . . ."[12] Now what is important is on the surface. Alon is certain that he discusses an account of words really said, of deeds truly done, on some one day, between two concrete, historical personalities. The story is history. Our work is to interpret the language and details of the story. Properly interpreted, these will tell us history: what Yoḥanan ben Zakkai did and why he did it, what Vespasian said and why he said it—on that day.

So the details of the story to which historians draw our attention concern what was said, what was done. In fact, as I shall now show, that is a false perspective on the character of each story. It presupposes that the story asks one set of questions, serves one set of purposes. But the story addresses a different purpose from the narrowly historical one. Each one is didactic. Each is an artifact of social culture and makes a point which is one representative of a social group, a fundamentally theological and secondarily exegetical lesson. The storyteller makes no pretense at narration of things which really happened. The reason is that his plan is to create not narrative but drama. He wishes not to tell a one-time event but to create a paradigm. In fact, as we shall now see, the story about Ḥoni portrays the relationship between the sage or rabbi and another type of heroic figure within the Jewish community, and the story about Yoḥanan ben Zakkai and Vespasian expresses the relationship between the sage or rabbi and another type of heroic figure among the nations of the world. So in their deepest structure both stories take up the problem of the relationship of a rabbi to another focus of power. As I shall spell out, each story answers the troubling question of how the rabbi relates to some other, competing type of powerful social character. The stories express the tension between rabbi and holy man, rabbi and emperor. They resolve that tension by explicit claims of priority for the source of the rabbi's power, knowledge of Scripture. The historical question to each is social. The issue unpacked through examining each is the mediation of social power ("at some one-time," "on that day" indeed!). Let me now spell this out.

V

STORY AND STRUCTURE

The importance of seeking the basic structure of a story is in discovering the essential purpose originally and perpetually served by the story. However interesting are matters of detail, it is when we can state the main point of a story that we enter into its meaning to the person who made it up. The beginning of interpretation lies not in explaining a mere detail, for instance, what Yoḥanan ben Zakkai really asked for, or really got, from Vespasian. The first and determinative step of interpretation is to find out the purpose of a story: the source of its conflict and resolution, the center of its action, the provocation of telling one detail and ignoring some other. These things we see when we uncover the basic, irreducible units through which the story unfolds. The power of a structuralist interpretation of literature is to chop away secondary matter and cut right to the heart. It is to uncover the logic of a story, unbound by context but timelessly revealed so that we, far away and long afterward, can see what the story originally meant (and may continue to mean). That is why so many find compelling the inquiry into structure and interpretation through canons of timeless logic. Structures by definition are timeless and enduring—the opposite of one-time events.

Now historians take for granted that the purpose of telling the tales before us is to relate things which really happened, one-time events, history as historians write it. We have therefore to ask whether the traits of the stories sustain this view. That is to say, when we look into the way in which the story is

told, do we discern an interest in an essentially one-time event?
To put matters simply: the point of entry is the focus of concern, the main point made by the story. I shall now show that both stories are so constructed as to do two things.

First, there is the principal purpose, which is didactic. The storyteller wishes to make certain points through *how* he tells the story. He is confident the person who hears or reads the story will grasp these points and so apprehend his purpose.[13]

Second, there is a secondary (but culturally primary) purpose, which is to link persons and events of the present age to those of Scripture. That is, the story not only has a didactic purpose, vis-à-vis the life of the community to which the story is addressed and for which it speaks. It also reveals a deeper, exegetical program, vis-à-vis the hero of the story itself. The true power of the rabbi lies in his knowledge of Scripture—and not in his power to work wonders or to dominate the affairs of nations and governments. Directed within the community of rabbis themselves, the stories project a picture of what a rabbi should be, which is a master of Scripture and of Torah, and show that through Scripture and Torah the rabbi can dispose of the conflicts of supernature and politics alike.

The inner structure of the story is blatant and expresses a highly conventional program. Only if we ignore that inner structure are we able to maintain that the story speaks once for all time, and not—as in fact it does—through lasting structures of recurrent events of power-relationships and enduring patterns of conflict. So the stories are not history, but old history newly reenacted. And, as I shall tentatively propose, Ḥoni emerges as a kind of Balaam, and Yoḥanan ben Zakkai, as a kind of Jeremiah. So "history" is told about what endures. That is, it is a kind of social science.

1. *The Structure of the Story about Ḥoni*

I discern four scenes in the story of Ḥoni, but the critical action takes place in a triad: three kinds of rain—too little, too much, just right but far too much. Everything else serves to set up this sequence of action or to make sense of it. These are the scenes.

(Scene One) They come to Ḥoni and say, "Pray for rain." He boasts: "Go take in the ovens so the clay will not soften in the rain—which I, Ḥoni, will now bring down by my prayers." What happens? Nothing.

(Scene Two) Ḥoni draws a circle and stands in the middle. He reminds God that the Israelites are God's children. Then he underlines who he, Ḥoni, is. He is a child of God more than the others. How so? "Everyone knows that I am like a member of the family before you." Ḥoni swears that he, the child of the family, will punish the head of the family. How? By standing in one spot until the head of the family does what Ḥoni demands. What happens? God plays a joke on Ḥoni: "It began to rain drop by drop."

(Scene Three) Honi complains that this is not the kind of rain that will move him outside of his circle. "This is not what I wanted!" So God plays another joke on Honi. God gives so much rain that the rain threatens to wash everything away—like the rain of the Flood in the time of Noah.

(Scene Four) Ḥoni complains again that this, too, is not the kind of rain he wanted. Now he gets what he wants. God's last joke on Ḥoni is that God still makes it rain too much. The people who came to Ḥoni to ask him to make it rain now come and tell him to make it stop raining. Ḥoni tries another boast: "Go see if a certain stone is under water." This is as if to say, "If the stone is now submerged, I'll turn off the rain." What happens? Nothing, just as at the outset. Now the story ends. Ḥoni leaves the action. This ending is extremely sudden. Honi now should do something else. Ḥoni does nothing. Why not? Because the point is clear.

The storyteller now makes a comment on the story. He needs no more evidence about Ḥoni. Ḥoni's true character and power, and God's opinion of Ḥoni, are self-evident. But the storyteller repeats in words the point he already has made in the actions and dialogues he has described. That is why we meet Simeon b. Shataḥ, a leading sage in the time in which Ḥoni is supposed to have lived. What Simeon says is pretty much what Ḥoni has said about himself. But he draws conclusions from the facts. He says that Ḥoni is indeed special. If anyone else tried Ḥoni's stunt, the sages would drive him away. But Ḥoni is what he says he is: "a spoiled child in the heavenly household." Then the storyteller concludes by citing a verse of Scripture that underlines the special, familial relationship between Ḥoni and Heaven.

The relevance of the biblical story of Balaam, prophet of the gentiles, is clear. Balaam enjoys a special relationship to God; he is a prophet. At the same time Balaam is the object of a joke on the part of Heaven. He goes to curse Israel, but ends up blessing them. He is a prophet who cannot even discern what a dumb ass can see. His power turns against himself. He is an object of ridicule. He who boasts that he can control Heaven is manipulated by Heaven—derisively so.

2. *The Structure of the Story about Yoḥanan ben Zakkai and Vespasian*

The first thing we must notice is that at the center and heart this is not a story about Yoḥanan ben Zakkai's escape from Jerusalem. That is not the source of the story's critical tension. The escape is not what makes the story work. The story is about the contrast between Yoḥanan ben Zakkai and Vespasian. Therein lies its generative tension. The story is long. But each part of it is needed. In fact, it is a play in five separate acts, two before the climax, which are matched against one another, then two after the climax, also matched against one another. And there is one in the middle—the climax of the whole story. Each scene is complete in itself. But one flows right on to the next. These "scenes" are conversations. At each point at which someone new begins to say something, we count a scene.

(Scene One) Vespasian talks to the inhabitants of Jerusalem. He tells them he simply wants them to submit. He will leave them alone. They tell him that they have done it before, and they can do it again.

(Scene Two) Yoḥanan ben Zakkai talks to the same people. Now he says to them, in the very same words, precisely what Vespasian said. He does make one important change. This shift is so important that the repetition of the same words as Vespasian said is absolutely essential to underline the differences. Vespasian called the people *fools*. Yoḥanan calls them *My children*. But the storyteller has precisely the same ending for both conversations. The people say the same words to Yoḥanan that they said to Vespasian. They see no difference between sage and general, life and death. This scene ends with a transition, a bridge between what has just happened and what is going to happen. Vespasian has "men inside the walls," spies. They write down on a piece of paper and shoot over the wall whatever they think Vespasian would want to hear.

(Scene Three) The next conversation is the climax of the story and makes its main point. People talk to one another in a dialogue. But the main point now is not the conversation but the scene itself. The scene is striking. Yoḥanan ben Zakkai

wants to get out of Jerusalem. The storyteller assumes we know
something he has not told, which is that one cannot walk out of
the city. He can get out only if he is dead. The reason—again,
we are not told—is that the people in control will not let anyone out. Since we already know that, so far as they are concerned, Yoḥanan ben Zakkai, the great sage, is no different from
Vespasian, the Roman general, we are prepared for this fact.
Yoḥanan lies down in the coffin. His students, Eliezer and
Joshua, carry out the coffin. The gatekeepers ask who is leaving, and they are told it is a corpse. They are treated like
ignorant people, "Do you not know. . . ." Once they are told
the facts, they let the coffin go through. Now Yoḥanan ben Zakkai
is brought to the Roman camp, right up to Vespasian's tent. Why
the Roman soldiers would let the Jewish sages carry a coffin
through their camp, and what they thought was happening, we are
not told. The storyteller will tell us only what we must know,
so that he can make his points through what he says, and through
what he does not say. The simple climax is that Yoḥanan rises
from the coffin. The coffin is for the dead. Yoḥanan has gone
down into death. And he has risen again, from the dead. He has
left the dying city, the city that soon will be dead and full of
corpses. He has come to the heart of the enemy's camp. There,
in the face of the cause of death, he rises from the dead. It is
a stunning set of contrasts, a long list of them. Then we have
two further conversations.

    (Scene Four) Yoḥanan and Vespasian talk. In fact, they
have two conversations. In the first one, Vespasian speaks first
and controls the conversation. In the second, Yoḥanan speaks
first and runs things. In the first conversation, Vespasian
recognizes Yoḥanan without being told. He immediately knows
it is Yoḥanan, which is why he asks whether it is Yoḥanan. If
he did not know it was Yoḥanan he would not have known to ask.
Then he wants to do something for Yoḥanan because Yoḥanan is
known as a friend of Vespasian. Yoḥanan asks for three little
things. He wants to go down to a coastal town named Yavneh,
which is no longer a battlefield. There he will (1) teach Torah
to his disciples. And he also will (2) establish a prayer house.
And, finally, he will (3) do all the commandments. In fact,
these three things sum up all of Judaism as the sages shape it.
Judaism is a religion that involves (1) study of Torah, (2) saying of prayers, and (3) doing all of the commandments. So these
"three little requests" to Vespasian are hardly so small as they
seem. But to Vespasian they will not appear great. For he is

engaged in a great war in the Land of Israel and a great adventure in Rome, as well. He wants to become emperor. He will be an important person. It is easy enough for him to do a little favor for Yoḥanan.

(Scene Five) At the end, Yoḥanan reciprocates and does a favor for Vespasian. It is also—in Yoḥanan's eyes—just as slight a favor for the Roman general as the right to go to Yavneh was in Vespasian's view. The thing that matters most to Yoḥanan is to go to Yavneh and there to teach his students and establish his prayer house and do the commandments. The thing that matters most to Vespasian is to become emperor. So Yoḥanan tells Vespasian that in a short time he will be made king. But the reason he will be made king, even though Vespasian does not know it, is Vespasian's position, here and now, before Jerusalem. Yoḥanan believes Vespasian is going to take Jerusalem. He therefore knows that Vespasian soon will be emperor. How does he know it? Because Yoḥanan is a master of the Torah. And in the Torah is a verse that says that "Lebanon" will fall by "a mighty one." Now in Yoḥanan's mind, "Lebanon" refers to the Temple. Perhaps this is because it was built out of cedars cut down in Lebanon and brought to Jerusalem in Solomon's time. Lebanon will fall to a mighty one—that is to say, in Yoḥanan's understanding of what Isaiah had said a long time ago, to an emperor or a king. So because of Yoḥanan's mastery of the Torah, he is able to tell Vespasian what is about to happen in faraway Rome. The end of this part of the story is predictable. What Yoḥanan said would happen did happen.

Now let us stand back and go over the five scenes of the play:

(One) Vespasian and the men of Jerusalem.
(Two) Yoḥanan ben Zakkai and the men of Jerusalem.
(Three) Yoḥanan lies down in a coffin and rises up from the coffin.
(Four) Vespasian does a favor for Yoḥanan, and gives him what he wants most of all.
(Five) Yoḥanan ben Zakkai does a favor for Vespasian, and gives him what he wants most of all.

So that is the story—a powerful and beautifully constructed drama. It would not be possible to tell the story more simply, or to say more things in the telling of it. The irony of the story is clear. Vespasian thought he was going to conquer the Jews. But the Jews came out able to rule themselves. Even though they ultimately gave over that bow and arrow, which meant

they accepted Roman rule, "our sages" saved them and organized a
government for them. Vespasian thought he was going to become
emperor because he was strong. But Yoḥanan ben Zakkai told him
the truth, which is that he would become emperor only because he
had the "merit" of taking Jerusalem and burning the Temple.
Yoḥanan was saying that the conqueror of the Temple was able to
do it because of one thing alone. God had permitted it. The
storyteller's secondary point comes at the end, when he has
Yoḥanan cite the verse of Isaiah to Vespasian. The storyteller
believes that Yoḥanan ben Zakkai knew what was going to happen
because Yoḥanan knew Scripture.

That brings up a second matter, the biblical passages of
which the tale reminds us, without citing them at all. Specifically, in the biblical book of Jeremiah, we see another example
of someone who in a time of siege tells the people to surrender.
Jeremiah believes that Nebuchadnezzar, king of the Babylonians,
is the rod of God's anger. He is going to take Jerusalem and
destroy the Temple because God wants to punish the Jews for their
sins. Jeremiah predicts that Jerusalem will fall to Babylonia.
Jeremiah Chapter Twenty shows Jeremiah is at odds with the Jeru-
salemites of his day. The same is clear in Chapter Twenty-one,
Chapter Twenty-two, and elsewhere in the prophecies of Jeremiah.
Further, when the Babylonians do take Jerusalem, Jeremiah is well
treated (Chapter Thirty-nine). And there is one final point.
Jeremiah makes provision for the future. He buys a piece of
ground, even when everyone thought it was all over for the people
of Israel in their Land. He did this to make sure people knew
there was hope and a future for the people and Land of Israel.
In the light of these passages in Jeremiah (and many others,
which say much the same thing), the story about Yoḥanan ben Zakkai
and his dealings with Vespasian takes on depth. We realize that
Yoḥanan is represented as a kind of Jeremiah, a living Scripture.

VI

AFTER STRUCTURALISM

Recognizing the structures of the narrative, perceiving
the didactic and polemical purpose served by each one, we stress
internal traits. That is how we have located those enduring
characteristics of structure and style which show us the logic
of the story. So we find ourselves wholly indifferent to a reading of the story as history. The story is something other than
history. Those who read this material as history misread the

purpose of the storyteller. Yet those who would abandon the historical dimension in interpreting these stories, who take up the structuralist position on interpreting them and treat them as utterly ahistorical, also err. It is not the naive and childish error of gullibility, such as historians of the old sort commit. It is error of a different order, as I shall now try to explain.

What is wrong with a mode of interpretation based principally upon the recognition of underlying structures of a story and leading to an ahistorical account of how the story works is that it is inadequate. Structuralism asks the right questions. It does not stand still to hear all the answers its questions precipitate. For if we conclude the work of interpretation with an account of the way the story is put together, we omit all reference to what remains critical in the interpretation of the story. To state matters simply: if we do not know who told a story, to whom, and for what purpose, if we cannot account for social context, we do not yet fully understand that story. Structure without context, that is, the social and economic, material context defined by concrete history, is insufficient either for description or for explanation.

Let me elaborate on this point. Internalistic, formal analysis is suggestive, but not exhaustive, of the layers of meanings of the story. Creations of literature express a logic unbound by context—but logic itself always is social and contextual. If we relativize all principles of analysis, we shall simply not fully make sense of the story we claim to interpret. There always are both diachronic and synchronic dimensions of interpretation, just as Schorske says. Nothing exists by itself. Someone tells a story. Someone hears, understands, and preserves it. Someone tells it later on. The very existence of sources for historical study bespeaks a historical process and a social continuum. That is why structuralism is impoverished—as much as is historicism.

We may amply describe a structure within the framework of religions and show how a system is constituted and how it functions. We may notice the fundamental concerns of the stories we have examined and show how the way in which the story is told highlights what the story wishes to tell us. But without careful attention to the historical context in which the story, as part of a system of values, actually functions, we still cannot explain what is important about the story. That is, we do not know how to describe and make sense of the system, the world-view and way of life, of which the story is a part. What is still more important, through (mere) structuralism we cannot account for changes within the system itself. Literature is part of society, and if we do not know what particular stimulus made it necessary or even inevitable that a story such as the one before us should be told, we cannot make sense of it.

Those structuralists who wish to provide systemic descriptions and literary analyses essentially outside the context of society and its history and change tell us something remarkably evanescent. They explain the condition of stasis. But ours is a world of change. Structuralism outside of the history of society and the framework of changing culture explains a system as it exists for a single moment. But systems unfold in history. True, the explanation is the thing. Out of structuralism come compelling explanations, stunning questions. But what is to be said of the explanation for the character of a system, when in yet a little while the system will change? Surely an explanation offered to account for the character of the system also must change. This means that the evidence of a system must be located, for interpretation, in the historical context of the social and material life of the people within the structure, in the present case, the people to whom the stories were told and who retell them.

So the challenge in reckoning with the sorts of tales before us is to move not merely past the ruins of historicism but beyond structuralism. A story of the ruined Temple or of drawing a circle and standing in it obviously is misread when narrowly historical questions define the mode of reading. The field of "Jewish history," consisting as it does in the discovery and recitation of facts (for ancient Judaism, pseudo-facts, in my view), is incompetent to deal with the sorts of tales we have read (and much else). But there is no salvation in structural anthropology and history of religions formed outside of a social, material context. That is so however much we must learn from those joined fields about the interpretation of facts, the description and analysis of systems, and the comparison of systems to systems, and of religions to religions. On the one side, history done by historians consists of accounts of one thing after another. On the other, history of religions yields vapid generalization. It often is helpless in the face of the specificities of facts and texts. Anthropology of religions, not unlike history, provides us with interminable catalogues of trivia on the one side, and compelling and enduring explanations of what are,

in fact, fleeting structures, on the other. So we stand between
the triviality of history and the evanescent taxonomy, divorced
from all context, of structuralism.[14]

I think in the end we have to find another way. For each
party performs a magic of reductionism. The historical side
effects the reduction of constants and structures to details. It
utterly misses the general in the search for the particular.
Event is made to exclude insight or to yield mere homily. The
one-timeness of historical narrative, the particularity and cultural narrowness of historical work, the focus on some few aspects
of a world and a system—these guarantee that history in its conventional mode will yield triviality. They assure it will collapse, as it does, into mindless antiquarianism. But the other
mode, the antihistorical description and interpretation effected
by structuralism reduces the flesh and blood of reality to neat
matchboxes ("grid-group" in Douglas is only a caricature of the
matter). Still, if I must choose, let my lot fall with the people
who take seriously the ebb and flow of time and society, who explain change and culture. The others essentially are reactionary.
For all their talk of deep structure, their taxonomies are profoundly irrelevant to the encounter with the world of material
reality and social being. Stories such as those before us emerge
from society and serve the purposes of society. They serve the
brokerage of power and speak of conflict. That may not be why
they were told to begin with; of that we cannot be certain. But
it certainly is society—a group of people—which preserved and
handed on these stories, and the reason is that society, a particular one of rabbis to be sure, understood and valued these
stories.

VII

STORY AS HISTORY IN ANCIENT JUDAISM

The analysis of the structure of the two stories indicates the purpose of the storyteller. It is not to report things
which really happened (surely an anachronism for ancient times),
but to make important points of a theological-didactic character.
Consequently, to adduce these stories in evidence of things which
really happened as these stories say they happened is absurd.
The reason is that the point of the story is missed, the wrong
question asked. To be sure, last-ditch defenders of the historicistic hermeneutic will invoke the distinction between the historical kernel of truth and the ahistorical husk of fable. But

that distinction, imposed on stories such as these, produces capricious and subjective results. Some people eat the kernel, while others (as in the case of Alon) swallow the husk too. Not only are we left without clear and consistent, systematic modes of reading these fables and tales. We also, and especially, as I have shown, focus on what is unimportant and miss what is important. Reading these stories as narrative history is wildly irrelevant to the point of the stories themselves. And, as I shall now suggest, it also obscures the kind of history the stories may be made to reveal, objectively, systematically, and consistently.

The two stories present history. It is a history of ideas and of religion, the history formed within the creative imagination of a group within Israelite society. If we know when, where, and to whom it was important to make up these two stories, we shall have insight into questions troubling the group which expressed itself through these stories. For what we have are statements of the system and structure of rabbis. The obvious purpose of the story about Ḥoni is to ridicule those whom rabbis envy, whose supernatural power they concede. Wonder-workers find no place within the rabbinical framework, for the reason expressed by Simeon b. Shataḥ's saying. The simple purpose of the story about Yoḥanan and Vespasian is to draw the contrast between the two sorts of powerful men, sage and emperor. So, as I said, at both sides of the margins of Israel the rabbi is represented as the dominant and critical figure. Within the community he confronts the miracle-worker. On the other side of the border he deals with another kind of power. He masters both, because in each case what he wants is what one should want—not the power over supernature enjoyed by Ḥoni, not the power over armies and empires enjoyed by Vespasian, but the power of the Torah which stands above supernature and nature.

Moving from these self-evident didactic purposes to the class or group of Israelite society represented by the stories, however, requires information not readily at hand. If we want accurately and fully to make sense of these stories as history, we have to locate the telling of the stories within history (when?), on the one side, and the preservation and retelling of them within a particular social group (by whom?), on the other. Let me ask some obvious questions to illustrate this point: When were miracle-workers a pressing problem to sages, so that a story about one of them would prove important? At what point did the rabbinical estate or movement become so remarkably self-conscious as to seek to locate itself at the limns, at the critical turning, of Israelite history? These two questions suggest what is needed to turn the stories into data for cultural and intellectual history. But it should be clear that the stories constitute not only artifacts of culture. They serve also to testify to social facts, to the material reality of relationships of institutions—rabbinical institutions. The storytellers speak of the exercise of power. Indeed, what makes the stories critical is their focus upon the two kinds of power rabbis in general did not exercise, supernatural and political. The power of the stories is their capacity to explain what kind of power rabbis do enjoy and why that sort of power is the most important sort. Since history is the tale of power and its disposition, these stories must stand as quintessentially historical facts.

Let me offer an example of how we might make use of those facts. It is meant to exemplify not results but modes of thought, ways of putting things together. If we postulate that polemic generally takes up threats near at hand, we must ask ourselves whether from the fact we may reconstruct the context.

In the case of a story about how miracle-working is true but undignified, we may wonder whether within rabbinical circles were men who aspired to validate rabbinical teachings through the making of miracles, as people said, for example, the teacher, Jesus, also was a wonder-worker. Since the story surfaces in the Mishnah, toward the end of the second century, we may notice that about second-century sages miracle stories are not told in the Mishnah, a document of that time, except for Ḥoni. But rabbis of the third, and more so, of the fourth century are widely portrayed as wonder-workers. Stories also are told in the strata of literature of that same later period about how first- and second-century rabbis did miracles.

In the case of a story about the rabbi and the emperor, we may, in like manner, wonder whether within rabbinical circles were men who aspired to vindicate rabbinical teachings through taking up political positions and forming an essentially political movement. Since the story surfaces in Abot deRabbi Natan, a secondary expansion of Abot ("the sayings of the fathers"), generally assigned to the period of the fourth or fifth century, we may notice that at precisely that same time a rapprochement appears to have taken place between the rabbinical estate of Babylonia and the exilarch who ruled the Jews of Babylonia with Iranian recognition. Rabbis of the later fourth and fifth centuries associated themselves with the exilarchate in ways in which those of the third and earlier fourth did not. Stories about hostility between rabbi and exilarch are told about figures of the earlier, not the later period.[15]

So one might speculate that both stories address for different periods growing tensions within the rabbinical circles themselves. Both take up positions against directions in which, in fact, the rabbinical movement for a time would move, toward wonder-working, toward politics. But both stories express the principal and ubiquitous value of the rabbinical movement, that is to say, the primacy and priority of Torah-learning. Both rapidly lose their narrow and polemical cloak. It goes without saying that these are mere suggestions of how to think about the tales in their social and historical context. If the proposed context changes, so will our speculation.

VIII

CONCLUSION

The stories focus upon the relationship of powerful people: rabbis and rain-makers, rabbis and emperors or generals. They mediate between the rabbis' kind of power and other kinds, acknowledged to be equally compelling. Telling these stories is urgent, specifically, in the society of rabbis or sages. The context of the telling and retelling is the larger setting of the life of the community of Israel, in which the rabbis claim, and eventually attain, considerable power of a material and substantial order. The tensions and contrasts which form the center of the two stories and make them work reveal facts about the social relationships in which those who told and heard the stories located themselves. A power other than supernatural or political, as represented by the rain-maker and the general, infuses the sage or rabbi. That power, the stories underline, derives from mastery of Scripture, of Torah. So far as history is the story of social conflict and the adjudication and mediation of diverse kinds of, and claims to, power, these stories tell us history. True, it is not, and cannot be, the history of a first-century B.C. wonder-worker or a first-century A.D. prophetic sage.

The story about Ḥoni surfaces in a document redacted at the end of the second century; the one on Yoḥanan first occurs in a document probably to be located in the fourth or fifth century. Some day, when we know more about Israelite society and its larger setting in these periods, as well as about the unfolding of the literature, institutions, and structures of the rabbinic estate and movement, we shall have access to still deeper layers of meaning, for a given place, time, and social group, contained and expressed in these stories. For these stories do constitute facts of history. If they are not factitious for the history of the period *of* which they speak, then they surely testify to the social relationships and imaginative life—the history—of the period(s) *to* which they speak.

NOTES TO CHAPTER ONE

[1] I cite and draw on Jonathan Z. Smith, "The Devil in Mr. Jones: Religion from the Perspective of the Human Sciences." Smith's address, given at the University of Chicago in his role as Dean of The College, will be published in a forthcoming book of essays in a series under my editorship. This paper served as the Spindel Memorial Lecture at Bowdoin College on October 5, 1980.

[2] Drawn from Smith.

[3] Carl E. Schorske, *Fin-de-siècle Vienna. Politics and Culture* (New York, 1980: Knopf), pp. xvii-xxii.

[4] Ibid., pp. xxi-xxii.

[5] Mishnah Taanit 3:8.

[6] Abot deRabbi Natan, Chapter Four.

[7] This is discussed, with full bibliography, in my *Life of Yohanan ben Zakkai*, 2d ed. (Leiden: E. J. Brill, 1970), pp. 145-73.

[8] William Dever, in *Biblical Archaeologist* 43, 1 (1980), 42.

[9] Joshua Trachtenberg, *Jewish Magic and Superstition* (Philadelphia: Jewish Publication Society of America, 1961), p. 121.

[10] Unsigned article, *Encyclopaedia Judaica* (Jerusalem: Keter, 1971), 8:964-65.

[11] Gedalyahu Alon, *Jews, Judaism and the Classical World* (Jerusalem: Magnes Press of the Hebrew University, 1977), p. 269.

[12] Ibid., pp. 294-95.

[13] So long as rabbinic culture remained intact, the storyteller was right. The stories were understood in exactly that context in which they originally were told, and for precisely that purpose for which the storyteller told them. Only when, in the nineteenth century, graduates of yeshivas entered universities to do Semitics or history were the stories asked to provide a kind of history which they never claimed to present. Read as history, the wrong details are interpreted. But historical questions are not wrong. They are merely irrelevant to the character of the data to which, in this instance, they are addressed. My students and I read a fair part of the literature of history founded on asking narrowly historical questions to Talmudic tales and fables and present the results in *The Formation of the Babylonian Talmud* (Leiden: Brill, 1971) and *The Modern Study of the Mishnah* (Leiden: Brill, 1973).

[14] That is, between the critics of Mary Douglas and Mary Douglas, so to speak. Her principal contribution, as I see it, is to insist on finding the principle of selection for a given system. This can be done for ancient Judaism represented by the Mishnah, as I have shown in my *Judaism: The Evidence of the Mishnah* (Chicago: University of Chicago Press, anticipated for 1981). But no "system" is isolated from the historical context defined by the on-going society framed and formed by said system. Douglas's taxonomic approach to the interpretation of Leviticus

seems to me sound, but her explanation of its systemic pertinence, that is, of the principle of selection, is too general. It therefore is inadequate to the sequence of contexts in which the taxonomy endured, even while the system changed. The strength of structuralism, as represented by Douglas, is its emphasis on the issue of discovering the principle of selection; the pathos is the incapacity to confront history—time and change in systems and societies. That is why the ultimate appeal is to rather self-evident generalities.

[15] My *History of the Jews in Babylonia* (Leiden: E. J. Brill, 1965-1970), I-V, presents extensive accounts of both wonder-working stories told about rabbis and stories expressive of hostility between exilarchs and rabbis. These are divided by periods (demarcated by the lives of the sages about whom they are told), and there clearly is a rise in the numbers of wonder-working tales from third through fifth centuries, on the one side, and a decline in the number of stories about hostility between rabbis and exilarchs, over the same period. Much more work is possible along these lines. And, of course, Abot deR. Natan to begin with is generally thought to be Palestinian and not Babylonian (!).

CHAPTER TWO

TOWARDS THE REHABILITATION OF TALMUDIC HISTORY

David Goodblatt
University of Haifa

I

Were I asked to define while standing on the proverbial one foot what are the topics on which I work, I would unhesitatingly reply: Talmudic history. If that one foot could stand the strain a little longer, I would explain that by Talmudic history I mean not the history of the Talmud, i.e., the literary critical study of the documents called the Talmud, but the Talmud as history, i.e., attempting to write history on the basis of Talmudic or rabbinic sources. (I am using the latter two adjectives interchangeably.) If that one-footed stance could be maintained still longer, I would add that by history I mean not intellectual history or the history of religion, but old-fashioned, "straight" history, the kind which deals with events, politics, institutions, and the like.

The statement that I work in Talmudic history may surprise people, for the latter discipline has come into some disrepute lately. In certain circles "Talmudic history" is a pejorative term, if not a dirty word. For example, it has been claimed that "the historical reading of the Babylonian Talmud and related literature . . . [is] essentially sterile. 'Talmudic history' is bankrupt of interesting questions and fructifying ideas."[1] Why would I want to associate myself with such an unpromising enterprise? Well, Talmudic history is the best brief description of the kind of work I do. It certainly is a more accurate label than rabbinics, or history of Judaism. Clearly, then, if I want to avoid embarrassment or the need for circumlocution when asked what my field is, I must seek the rehabilitation of Talmudic history. And what better place to begin my campaign than the Max Richter Conversation on the History of Judaism. My contribution toward the rehabilitation of Talmudic history will have three parts. First, I shall try to answer some of the general objections leveled against this field of study. Second, I shall discuss how Talmudic history can properly be done. In discussing methodology I shall touch on some of the more important advances in this field in recent years. Third, having convinced you that Talmudic history is both legitimate and possible, I shall try to explain why it is interesting and important. By treating these issues I shall at the same time be answering the questions posed by Professor Neusner in his invitation to the Conversation.

II

My attempted rehabilitation of Talmudic history begins with a response to the criticism of this field appearing in Professor Neusner's provocative *Method and Meaning in Ancient Judaism*. That criticism is summarized in an introductory section from which I have already quoted the charge that Talmudic history is sterile, bankrupt, and dull. Following this charge are three more detailed criticisms which I shall take up in order. The passage continues:

> More than a century has been spent on the question: What went on in the time of the Talmud? But the question is poorly framed. First, the Talmud does not define an age, though it is a definitive document. For historical purposes, however, it is merely another source.[2]

So far the first criticism, which appears to be an objection to the use of the concept "the period of the Talmud." But, to begin with, the periodization of history by cultural criteria can be paralleled from other, respectable, branches of history. Witness the age of the Renaissance, the Romantic era, New Testament times, etc. Moreover, I believe that "the period of the Talmud" is a perfectly respectable, convenient, and neutral way to refer to the period in which the Talmud (or rabbinic literature) came into being and about which it testifies. Of course I am well aware that by common consent and in all probability that period overlaps with the Roman and Byzantine era in Palestine, the late Parthian and Sasanian eras in Babylonia, and depending on how we define rabbinic literature, probably the ʿUmayyad eras in both countries. But notice how long and cumbersome the last sentence was. And notice that the periods overlap; they are not coterminous. Is it not more convenient simply to say "the period of the Talmud." One might also refer to centuries, say Palestine in the third and fourth centuries. But to refer to well-defined dates requires the precise solution of problems of provenance that I doubt are soluble. Hence my preference for a noncommittal phrase like "the period of the Talmud." In any case, Talmudic historians have no real stake in what one calls the period about which we write. Indeed, that period defines us only accidentally, not essentially. What really defines the Talmudic historian is the fact that he specializes in the use of certain sources, viz., rabbinic literature. So if our colleagues feel more comfortable when we speak of late antiquity, or the late empire, I think we can oblige. And certainly a dislike for the concept "the period of the Talmud" does not prove the illegitimacy of Talmudic history.

The next two criticisms are more substantial and to the point. Our passage continues:

> Second, what is important to the Talmud itself—what the Talmud is about—is not the stories told quite *en passant*, the tales of saints, kings, exilarchs, rabbis, teachers, disciples, and judges. These materials answer important questions. But the questions are not about what things really were like in the centuries in which the Talmud was taking shape.[3]

If I understand this argument correctly, it proceeds from what I take to be an undeniable fact: rabbinic literature is not an historiographic work. That is, it does not intend to tell us about what was going on when it was composed. It is not interested in recording the events and institutions witnessed by its creators. But does this fact mean that the Talmud can tell us nothing about what things were like when it was taking shape? Or, to put matters more generally, must the historian limit himself to only those sources which are themselves historiographic in character? Such a rule would be the historian's version of the genetic fallacy. After all, an artifact may fulfill functions other than those for which it was crafted--one thinks of the blunt instrument of detective fiction. So too may a written source tell us much more than, or something different from, what its author intended. I doubt whether even the historians of modern times, swamped though they are by sources, would be willing to adopt such a restrictive rule of evidence. How much more so the student of ancient times who gladly accepts every scrap of information which has survived from antiquity, be it as humble as a tax bill or a sales receipt. In sum, whatever the intent of its creators, rabbinic literature is full of information about what was going on in the time in which it came into being. To be sure, that information is very unevenly distributed over a wide range of topics. Often we have the most information about topics we are uninterested in, and the least about those which interest us greatly. But given the extent of our ignorance, we cannot afford to give up whatever information the Talmud contains. And,

as I shall briefly indicate below, that information is often
unique, not just for the history of the Jews, but also for the
history of antiquity in general.

I come now to the third objection to Talmudic history.
Our passage continues:

> Third, the critical issues of history cannot be worked
> out along presently available lines. If, for example,
> we cannot demonstrate that a given authority really
> said what is attributed to him, then we cannot write
> his intellectual biography. If we cannot demonstrate
> that he really did what he is said to have done, then
> we cannot write his biography in material and concrete
> terms either. It follows that the Talmud does not per-
> mit us to report about the doings of the men who are
> its heroes, about the practical consequences of the
> teachings which are its purpose and its point, nor
> about the age in which it came into being and about
> which it speaks.[4]

This final criticism also proceeds from what I take to be a fact.
This is the impossibility of writing biographies, intellectual or
otherwise, about the masters named in the Talmud. But does it
follow from this that "the Talmud does not permit us to report
. . . about the age in which it came into being and about which
it speaks"? Our inability to write biography does not mean we
cannot write history. There are other kinds of historical
inquiry aside from biography, and in addition to the history of
ideas and religion. And as I shall show in the next section, at
least some issues of critical history can be and are being
worked on along presently available lines. In short, the impossibility of rabbinic biography does not entail the impossibility
of Talmudic history.

After responding to the three general criticisms of Talmudic history, I hope I have demonstrated that there is nothing
inherently and in principle illegitimate in the attempt to use
rabbinic sources in writing history. However, the legitimacy in
principle of Talmudic history does not guarantee that this enterprise is either feasible in practice or capable of producing
significant results. That it is, in fact, both feasible and
productive is the burden of the next two sections.

III

As already mentioned, people have been doing Talmudic
history for over a century. And the results have been disap-
pointing, But are the results in other areas of study related
to rabbinic literature much better? And while Talmudic history
has had many inept practitioners, I doubt whether one could say

that it has had more than its share. In any event, however bad the past, what has been is not what has to be. In fact, in recent years Talmudic history has moved out in new, more promising directions, escaping from the dead ends in which many of the earlier practitioners had trapped themselves. In less picturesque language, there have been a number of methodological advances in recent Talmudic history, some of which I shall now discuss.

Perhaps the single most important development is what one might call the debiographization of rabbinic literature (and consequently of Talmudic history). By this I mean the recognition, alluded to above, that the narratives and anecdotes about the masters cannot be taken as historical, literally true biographical information. This conclusion has been arrived at by a number of scholars working on different approaches to rabbinic literature, though not all their arguments are of equal weight or application. I would mention here the history of tradition work of Professor Neusner and his students and the somewhat similar work of Peter Schäfer, the comparative literary work of classicists like E. E. Halevy and especially Henry Fischel, and the structuralist analyses of folklorists like Dan Ben-Amos and Dov Noy and of the Talmudist Yonah Fraenkel. Fortunately I need not go into detail since I can refer those interested to the admirable article by W. S. Green, "What's In a Name?"[5]

The conclusion that rabbinic biography is not possible invalidates much of the older Talmudic history (and some recent work too). One need only skim the relevant chapters of Graetz, Weiss, Halevy—to say nothing of Bacher—to see how much of their work is biographical in character. Even as sophisticated an historian as Alon often builds on a biographical framework. But the important point is that the abandonment of rabbinic biography has a positive, as well as a negative, effect. It can be a liberating experience, freeing the Talmudic historian from the pursuit of wills-of-the-wisp like "the historical Yohanan ben Zakkai." The energies released from such vain pursuits may now be devoted to other kinds of questions, questions that the sources are capable of answering. And when one surveys some of the recent work in Talmudic history, one notices that there has, in fact, been a movement away from biography into other areas.

The movement in new directions is symbolized by the title of a recent book, A. Amir's *Institutions and Titles in Talmudic Literature* (Jerusalem, 1977). And it is illustrated by such books as Sperber's two monographs on money and land, by M. Beer's book on the socioeconomic status of the Babylonian Amoraim, by my own work on academic institutions, by such studies of realia as those of Brand on ceramics and glass, and those of Feliks on agriculture.[6] To be sure, the abandonment of biography and the concentration on other kinds of inquiry do not guarantee the quality of the work. The uncritical use of sources, for example, is not limited to biographers nor is it the exclusive domain of the "straight" historians either as we shall see below. Still in all, the debiographization of Talmudic history is a very encouraging development.

The recent work I just referred to suggests the kinds of historical issues available to the Talmudic historian: social and economic history, institutions, realia, and one should add historical geography. But I doubt whether it is possible to list in advance all of the historical issues which the Talmud can illuminate. What really counts is the principle involved, viz., we cannot study anything we want. Rather we must abandon those issues on which our sources cannot inform us, such as the biography of Aqiba, and discover the questions which our sources can answer for us. This principle is one of the two pillars on which Talmudic history stands. The other pillar is the need to locate the information which the sources do provide in its proper geographical and chronological setting. And this means, in most cases, determining the provenance of the sources. This aspect of Talmudic history has also seen considerable progress in recent years.

Some of this progress has taken away as much as it has given. For example, Professor Neusner has persuasively argued that much of the Mishnah was composed simultaneously with its redaction. If this is correct, then the Mishnah is much less useful a source for the second century than we had thought. At the same time, its importance for the early third century increases. In other areas progress has been uniformly positive. This is especially true for the Babylonian Talmud. When I began to work on Talmudic history a decade ago, I had to acknowledge that my dating of the sources was highly speculative. By dating materials attributed to named Babylonian masters to the half century within which they flourished I was relying on several unproved assumptions. One was that the Babylonian Talmud is not the work of a sixth- or seventh-century pseudepigrapher, but that it actually preserves sources composed in different periods. Another assumption was that the sources from different periods were preserved materially intact in form and language, and that they were not "homogenized" by later editors. A mere decade ago these were reasonable, but still unproved assumptions. Today I can say that they are facts.

It is the literary critics to whom we are indebted for the demonstration that the Babylonian Talmud is not a sixth- or seventh-century pseudepigraph. They have shown that the latter document contains a sizeable post-Amoraic stratum which is recognizable by such objective criteria as terminology, language (i.e., grammar and vocabulary), literary form, and fluidity of text tradition. Among other features, the post-Amoraic stratum is anonymous, i.e., not attributed to named authorities--aside from a few, easily discernible glosses inserted into attributed material. This means that the attributed material, and unattributed material which shares other features of the former, can confidently be assigned to the third through the fifth centuries rather than to the sixth and seventh. And this already tells us that the final editors of the Babylonian Talmud did not attempt to "homogenize" the two strata, but rather left the Amoraic material essentially intact.[7]

But what about the Amoraic stratum itself. Can we date its contents to specific generations within the Amoraic era? For example, do the third-century masters speak differently than the fourth-century ones? Or do they all speak with one voice and in one style—a sure sign of the heavy hand of an editor. In this case it is the Talmudic historians themselves who have resolved this question. They have established that it is possible to distinguish between earlier and later sources within the Amoraic stratum. To illustrate with an example which is very familiar to me, the third-century masters do not mention the same academic institutions as the fourth- and fifth-century masters do. Since the former do mention (other) academic institutions, this difference in terminology is not likely to be accidental. And since the later stratum of the Babylonian Talmud is unaware of this difference, it is not likely to be the work of a tendentious editor. Instead, the most likely explanation is that the terminology of third-century sources has been accurately preserved, which terminology reflects the institutional structure existent in the third century.[8] To generalize, it appears that the language of the different generations of the Babylonian Amoraim was not "homogenized" by the editors of the Babylonian Talmud. (Some "homogenization" did take place in the post-redactional transmission of the text, but this is usually revealed by a study of the text tradition.) On the whole the compilers of the Babylonian

Talmud appear to have preserved the earlier (Babylonian) sources essentially intact in form and language.

The developments just summarized mean that we can now date many of the sources in the Babylonian Talmud with considerable confidence and with some precision. And our ability reliably to date the sources means that our historical work will be on firmer footing. Of course, I have discussed only the Babylonian Talmud. But I suspect that similar results will be forthcoming from a study of the Palestinian Talmud which is so similar in form to the Amoraic stratum of the Babylonian. More difficult is the case of the midrashic literature, which is so rich in anecdotal and narrative material. It seems clear that the various collections of midrashic material contain sources which antedate the time of redaction of the collections. But how can we determine the date of the earlier materials? This is a problem still awaiting its solution.[9] Perhaps the philologists will be able to help. Their distinction between Middle Hebrew[1] and Middle Hebrew[2] may enable us to identify genuinely Tannaitic sources even in late compilations.[10] And in any case, sometimes even the grossest distinctions, such as between Tannaitic and Amoraic sources, or between Palestinian and Babylonian, can yield significant results for the historian.[11]

In sum, determining the provenance of the sources and discovering which questions the sources can answer, this is the whole strategy of Talmudic history. The rest is just tactics to be worked out in practice according to the specific selection of sources involved and the particular questions being asked. Recent years have seen progress on both aspects of this strategy. The demise of rabbinic biography has helped move Talmudic historians away from questions our sources cannot answer. And at least in some cases we have discovered that we can reliably date our sources. So whatever the mistakes of the past—or the present—I believe that Talmudic history can be and often is methodologically respectable.

IV

Granted that Talmudic history can be methodologically respectable, is it capable of producing interesting and important results? I find this question hard to answer, for I have always been under the impression that importance is a relative (or do I mean relational) category and interest a subjective one. Thus it is obvious that the student of the history of the Jews in Sasanian Babylonia will find Talmudic history both interesting and important. Indeed, such a person has nowhere else to turn. And though in less desperate straits, the student of the history of the Jews in Roman-Byzantine Palestine will also depend on Talmudic history. Even less parochial historians of antiquity are likely to find the results of Talmudic history significant. For example, it turns out that the Babylonian Talmud is the single most extensive source on Sasanian taxation prior to the sixth-century reforms of Khusro I.[12] And Daniel Sperber has suggested that Talmudic history may help supply a corrective to the papyri-induced Egyptocentrism of much recent socioeconomic history of the Roman empire.[13]

However, since this Conversation is devoted to the history of Judaism, I would like to show how Talmudic history is interesting and important for the historian of religion working on rabbinic sources. I shall aruge that it is difficult to do the history of Talmudic Judaism without the assistance of Talmudic history. In fact, I believe this last statement is so obvious as to be a truism. First of all, all aspects of the study of rabbinic sources are interrelated. Talmudic historians, for example, are very dependent on the work of the text critics and philologists. Second, the interrelationship between a given religious system and its social and historical matrix has been argued by many scholars, most recently by Professor Neusner in his discussion of the ecology of religion.[14] Thus it is a priori likely that the Talmudic historian will have something of significance to say to the historian of Judaism.

The significance of Talmudic history becomes clear when we remember that the statement that, say, the second-century masters believed X is as much an historical assertion as is the statement that Aqiba did or said something. In both cases it is the task of the Talmudic historian to ask how, or even whether, we can know that such an assertion is correct. What happens when this kind of question is either not asked or nor properly answered may be seen in two recent studies: Urbach's *The Sages* and Sandmel's *Judaism and Christian Beginnings*. I need not repeat here the critique of these books by Professor Neusner, who documents their uncritical, i.e., ahistorical, use of rabbinic sources.[15] Instead I would stress that both these books belong to the category of history of Judaism, not Talmudic history. In fact, it is precisely the failure of Urbach and Sandmel to make use of critical Talmudic history which so detracts from their attempt to write an accurate history of Judaism.

Allow me to adduce one more example of how significant Talmudic history can be for the history of Judaism. It is universally assumed that the Mishnah was compiled and published in the early third century. Consequently it is also universally agreed that the Mishnah is our earliest extant rabbinic document. As such it obviously is our single most crucial source for the history of early rabbinic Judaism. And just as obviously a correct understanding of the meaning of this document requires as full as possible an understanding of the social and historical matrix from which it emerged, and of the intention of its authors so far as we can recover this. For example, there is the long-standing debate among the Talmudists as to whether the Mishnah was intended to be a law code or a school textbook.[16] I am not sure how, or whether, this question can be resolved. But I am sure of two things. First, I believe that this question is an historical one. And second, if we cannot decide whether or not the Mishnah is a law code, then we also cannot decide whether or not the Mishnah was intended by its authors to "contain the most important things they could specify."[17] Clearly we shall be impeded in our attempt to understand the meaning of the document so long as we are not able to resolve these issues.

Let us explore the implications of the life setting and original purpose of the Mishnah for its interpretation. If this document was intended to be (merely) a law code, then the information which the historian of religion may derive from it is rather circumscribed. Its detailed laws will probably reflect not the theology or ideology of its authors, but rather the accidents of legal history and interpretation. After all, this is the case even with that most philosophical of all Jewish law codes, the Mishneh Torah of Maimonides. Now I certainly do not mean to assert that the Mishneh Torah is devoid of philosophy. But suppose the Maimonidean controversy of the thirteenth century had ended in the triumph of the antiphilosophic party who were then able to suppress the Guide for the Perplexed and the first of the fourteen books of the Mishneh Torah. If we had only the last thirteen books of the latter code, would we be able to deduce from it the theology of Maimonides? Could we reconstruct from the details of his laws on the mixing of milk and meat his theory of the active intellect? Obviously not. But I wonder whether we would even have a fair idea of Maimonides' religious position. Certainly nothing in the Mishneh Torah would prepare us for the rather lowly position assigned to experts in the halakhah, even such as have correct theological notions on the basis of tradition, in the famous parable of the palace in the latter part of the third section of the Guide.

I can supplement the example from Maimonides with one involving collective works. I refer to two documents written within a dozen years of each other in the same place and by many of the same people: the Declaration of Independence and the Constitution of the United States. Now I think that a student of the political philosophy of the founding fathers who relied solely on the Constitution would be led seriously astray. In any case, could he deduce from the Constitution, with its recognition of slavery and its counting of slaves as three-fifths of a person, that its authors believed that all men were created equal with inalienable rights to liberty and the pursuit of happiness? Of course, the historians could explain the different purposes of the two documents and the different circumstances in which each was written. Similarly, to revert to Maimonides, there are various theories explaining the discontinuities between his Mishneh Torah and his Guide, aside from the obvious ones involving the different purposes of each book.

It may be objected that my examples from Maimonides and the founding fathers are misleading. If the Mishnah is claimed to be analogous to the Mishneh Torah and the Constitution, then what is the early rabbinic analogue to the Guide for the Perplexed and the Declaration of Independence? An obvious answer would be the homiletic and gnomic material attributed to the same masters to whom the legal traditions of the Mishnah are assigned. And if one objects that much of this nonlegal material appears only in documents redacted much later than the Mishnah, then I would reply that such material also appears in the Mishnah itself. Granted the latter document contains only a limited amount of homiletic and gnomic sources—though there is an entire tractate, Avot, devoted to it. Still, such material is not absent. And, at the very least, this proves that the authors of the Mishnah were perfectly capable of speaking directly about matters of religion and theology. And this in turn suggests that when they do not directly speak of such matters—as is usually the case in the Mishnah—then they may well have other things on their mind. Obviously, I cannot resolve here the questions I have just raised about the intention of the authors of the Mishnah. I merely wished to show that until Talmudic history gives us a clearer understanding of the life setting and original purpose of the Mishnah, the historian of religion will find it difficult to interpret its meaning.

At this point my attempts to rehabilitate Talmudic history may come to an end. Ultimately that rehabilitation depends on our recognition that the study of rabbinic literature cannot be the exclusive preserve of any one discipline, be it literary criticism, linguistics, law, religion, or history. Each of these disciplines has its own contribution to make, but at the same time each one depends on the others. Nor can any of these disciplines be dismissed as uninteresting, for there will always be certain temperaments attracted to each of them. And, finally, if the Talmud is more resistant to the inquiry of the historian than it is to the inquiries of other disciplines, well may we quote from the words of the masters: *lefum ṣa'ara agra.*

NOTES TO CHAPTER TWO

[1] Jacob Neusner, *Method and Meaning in Ancient Judaism* (Missoula, Mont., 1979), p. 6.

[2] Ibid., pp. 6-7.

[3] Ibid., p. 7.

[4] Ibid.

[5] W. S. Green, "What's In a Name?—The Problematic of Rabbinic 'Biography,'" in *Approaches to Ancient Judaism: Theory and Practice*, ed. W. S. Green (Missoula, Mont., 1978), pp. 77-96. Green cites most of the relevant literature. Add J. Fraenkel, "Hermeneutic Problems in the Study of the Aggadic Narrative," *Tarbiz* 47 (5738), 139-72, and Peter Schäfer, *Studien zur Geschichte und Theologie des rabbinischen Judentums* (Leiden, 1978), Introduction and passim.

[6] M. Beer, *The Babylonian Amoraim. Aspects of Economic Life* (Ramat Gan, 1974); A. Ben-David, *Talmudische Ökonomie. Die Wirtschaft des jüdischen Palästina zur Zeit der Mischna und des Talmud*, 1 (Hildesheim und New York, 1974); Y. Brand, *Ceramics in Talmudic Literature* (Jerusalem, 1953) and *Glass Utensils in Talmudic Literature* (Jerusalem, 1978), Y. Feliks, *Agriculture in Palestine in the Period of the Mishnah and Talmud* (Jerusalem, 1963); D. Goodblatt, *Rabbinic Instruction in Sasanian Babylonia* (Leiden 1975); D. Sperber, *Roman Palestine 200-400. Money and Prices* (Ramat Gan, 1974) and *Roman Palestine 200-400. The Land* (Ramat Gan, 1978).

[7] See my article, "The Babylonian Talmud," in *Aufstieg und Niedergang der römischen Welt*, II, 19, 2 (Berlin and New York, 1979), pp. 294-95, 300-301, 314-18, and the works cited there.

[8] See D. Goodblatt, *Rabbinic Instruction in Sasanian Babylonia* in connection with the terms *kallah*, *pirqa*, and *rosh yeshivah/resh metivta*. For independent confirmation see Y. Gafni, "Yeshivah and Metivta," *Zion* 43 (5738), 12-37.

[9] See the discussion in Schäfer, *Studien*.

[10] On this see the summary in Goodblatt, "The Babylonian Talmud," pp. 277-78, and especially the references to the work of Sokoloff and Moreshet.

[11] See, for example, D. Goodblatt, "The Beruriah Traditions," *Journal of Jewish Studies* 27 (1975), 68-85.

[12] See my article, "The Poll Tax in Sasanian Babylonia: The Talmudic Evidence," *Journal for the Economic and Social History of the Orient* 22 (1979), 233-95.

[13] See Sperber, *The Land*, Introduction.

[14] See Jacob Neusner, *The Way of Torah*, 3d ed. (Belmont, Calif., 1979), pp. xi-xiv.

[15] On Sandmel see Neusner, *Method and Meaning*, pp. 26-27. On Urbach see J. Neusner, "The Sages, Beliefs and Opinions by Ephraim E. Urbach," *Journal of Jewish Studies* 27 (1976), 23-35.

[16] See the opinions in J. Neusner, ed., *The Modern Study of the Mishnah* (Leiden, 1973).

[17] Cf. Neusner, *Method and Meaning*, p. 28.

CHAPTER THREE

A NEW APPROACH TO EARLY JEWISH PRAYER

Tzvee Zahavy
University of Minnesota

Prayer is the central phenomenon of religion, the very hearthstone of all piety.
Friedrich Heiler, *Prayer*
(Oxford, 1932, p. 1)

I

THE PROBLEM

The study of prayer[1] is an urgent concern for the analysis of religion. Prayer is an unquestionably religious activity[2] central to religion in two distinct ways. First, it represents a significant ritual or set of activities; as such it is important to the *way of life* of any religious system. Second, the utterances of those praying, or prayer-texts, often express significant conceptions of cosmology and theology—ideas which convey conceptions of meaning and beliefs expressive of the *worldview* of a religious system.

The study of prayer throws light on late antique Judaism and later religious phenomena. Rabbinic Judaism is one Judaic religious system which takes shape between the first and fifth centuries C.E. Hence the study of early Judaic prayer, especially its rabbinic forms, will help us understand the formation of rabbinic Judaism. In addition, later Judaic prayer down to the present adheres to the framework for prayer established in the Tannaitic period.[3] Thus study of the earliest manifestations of this foundation may contribute to our understanding of the later development of Judaic prayer. Moreover, it is commonly assumed that early Christian prayer bears some relationship to its Judaic counterpart. If so, the study of early rabbinic prayer may shed some light on the development and character of early Christian religion and literature.[4]

With the importance of the analysis of early rabbinic prayer thus established it is next necessary to spell out in what ways one may undertake the general study of prayer. In the initial stage of this undertaking one must distinguish among the distinct aspects of the phenomenon under scrutiny. In this instance there are at least three separate major concerns. First, the analysis of *prayer* may involve the study of *prayer-texts*,

standardized liturgical compositions. Second, those who study
the phenomenon of *prayer* should, where possible, inquire into
acts of *praying* which may include the investigation of the material context and trappings of its rituals. Finally, the third
issue of the study of this phenomenon is the analysis of those
statements which develop metaphysical or philosophical concepts
of Judaism based on an understanding either of texts of prayer or
of the act of praying. Methods for pursuing the investigation of
these three distinct facets of prayer must be drawn from several
independent disciplines or subdisciplines of the history of religions. It is thus necessary next to spell out in some greater
detail the diverse methods and problems pertinent to research
into early rabbinic prayer. That is the primary issue which I
address. The secondary concern which I take up at my conclusion
is whether a coherent and integrated interdisciplinary study of
this phenomenon of religion is feasible and, if so, how the
results of such an inquiry will further our knowledge of the
history of Judaism.

II

THE PRAYER-TEXTS

Let us begin by discussing the *prayer-texts*. The methods
which one employs to study these standardized liturgical compositions, as with each of the three aspects of prayer, are determined by the nature of the evidence in question. The extant
early rabbinic prayer-texts do not come to us as actual material
remains of the past. Rather the alleged early rabbinic liturgic
compositions are transmitted within literary traditions. These
appear in two forms. First, in rabbinic compilations we find a
few scattered, sometimes fragmentary, prayer compositions.[5] The
value of this derivative evidence, which comes to our hands via
repeated recopying, is difficult to assess. Though we presume
scribes copy texts accurately, for prayer-texts, some of which
are in common use in medieval Jewish liturgy, the likelihood is
great that later scribes maintain the literary tradition in line
with prevailing practice.

Our second literary source of liturgic texts is the
standardized prayerbook. Many recent monographs make implicit
and explicit assertions and assumptions that liturgic standardization predates the earliest publication of a formal order of
prayers[6] and goes way back to the Tannaitic or Amoraic period.
The recent work of L. A. Hoffman corrects this methodological
imprecision. In his monograph on *The Canonization of the*

Synagogue Service, he examines the "geonic attempt at liturgical standardization."[7] His cogent characterization of the status of formalized liturgy in the earlier Talmudic period summarizes his view of the limits of our knowledge of this matter:

> . . . There is justification for conceding not only that the Talmud delineates no all-inclusive set of prescribed wording for prayers but even that it lacks evidence of the logically prior step: rabbinic consensus on what prayers there are for which common words might be sought. Beyond a common vocabulary that signifies a generally accepted framework in which licit worship might proceed, the rabbis could come to little agreement on what was proper and what not. This is a liturgical license which modern standards might even brand as chaotic. The majority of rabbinic debates end in no clear decision at all, and there is no evidence to indicate that even those debates which are resolved had any success in converting popular practice one way or another.[8]

Hoffman signals a number of cautions for future research into Judaic liturgy in late antiquity each of which has been ignored in the past by one or more scholars writing on the subject. He correctly questions the existence at that early time of a uniform liturgy,[9] and of the import and effectiveness of the limited rabbinic consensus on proper liturgic practice.[10]

Less cautious scholars have drawn conclusions which differ from Hoffman's. Many make assumptions about the existence of standardized liturgic texts, about uniform rabbinic rites of prayer, and about the role of rabbinic legislation in regulating liturgic conformity.[11] Some writers have gone on to speculate further on the nature of the social or political situations which lead to the creation of a given formalized text or to the implementation of a particular standardized rite.[12] Such speculation built upon uncertainty leads only to doubtful conclusions. It surely does not assist us in focusing with precision on and interpreting the meaning of the limited evidence which we have of liturgic activity of this early period.

There are yet further methodological hurdles to clear in understanding the nature of the liturgic legacy of early rabbinic Judaism. Once we critically and cautiously establish the canons of our data of this elusive subject and sidestep the temptation to project medieval or modern conditions of liturgic development into late antique Judaism, we may then go on to interpret the substantive meaning of the evidence. That is to say, through critical inquiry we may seek to know a significant amount about the worldview inherent in early rabbinic prayer. But it may be difficult to establish with certainty what the evidence tells us about the early rabbinic religious system and its development. The data which we have may be amenable to several varying but equally plausible interpretations. Each of these may suggest a totally distinctive conclusion about the essential conceptual nature of the worldview of early rabbinic Judaism. One example will demonstrate the uncertainty of a straightforward phenomenological inquiry into our evidence. It seems quite likely that the *shema'* was central to early rabbinic liturgy.[13] It is proper then to ask about the essential meaning of this prayer which cites Deut. 6:4-9, Deut. 11:13-21, Num. 15: 37-41. Does the citation of these passages indicate the early rabbinic assertion of the centrality of a monotheistic creed, as is commonly assumed? Or can the case be made for interpreting the liturgic use of these verses as statements on the importance of prophylactic religious objects such as phylacteries, fringes, and door amulets and of the power of God's name to protect the faithful Israelite? Perhaps both alternatives are at once plausible. In any case it is clear that the essential interpretation of what limited evidence we have of the early rabbinic era will inform us of central elements of the worldview of this religious system. In some ways though this endeavor is problematic, as the critical phenomenological analysis of the limited repertoire of early rabbinic prayers and their themes may not lead to conclusive unidimensional results. Nonetheless this mode of inquiry is a *sine qua non* to our understanding of the development of rabbinic Judaism.[14]

The *prayers*, and especially the blessings, which we can establish with some certainty existed early on, will be of significant value for the study of Judaism and, as I indicated at the very outset, perhaps of early Christianity as well. Now a number of issues yet remain to be addressed to further inform the study of early rabbinic *prayer*. Paramount among these is the question of how these texts or liturgic formulae were used in rabbinic life. We turn then next to the second facet of our concern--the study of *praying* in late antique rabbinic Judaism.

III

ACTS OF PRAYING: MATERIAL REMAINS

Naturally, in attempting to describe what we can know of rabbinic Jews at prayer we are again constrained by the nature of our evidence. Unfortunately we have no equivalent for late antique Judaism of Heilman's anthropological study of modern American synagogue life.[15] The primary testimonies from antiquity which refer to Jews in general at prayer are few and far between and are, if not hostile,[16] at best anecdotal.[17] If we are to utilize the episodic literary evidence for composing a picture of late antique rabbinic Jews at prayer we need to establish the contextual meaning of each relevant pericope whether in early rabbinic, Qumran, Apocrypha and Pseudepigrapha, or early Christian literature. Then we may perhaps establish the outlines of our knowledge based on the literary testimonies. Once again we ought to exercise caution in using literary traditions and be alert for both the *tendenz* of the original source and the possibility of scribal alteration in transmission of the document.[18]

Material remains of the period are another potential source of primary evidence on the nature of early Jewish prayer. These data are in some ways more reliable than literary traditions as evidences. The ritual objects used in prayer and the numerous synagogue sites which have been discovered and analyzed presumably stand as eyewitnesses to Jewish prayer in late antiquity. Unfortunately it is difficult for us to elicit direct answers to critical questions from these mute witnesses. Can synagogue stones and structure tell us who prayed within their walls? Can phylacteries and scrolls tell us who used them? Is it possible to determine whether those who left us these remains were members of early rabbinic society? Did the Jews who worshipped in ancient synagogues recite those texts of prayer which we have alluded to above?[19] Did they propound those conceptions of prayer and society which rabbinic tractates preserve for us?[20]

The material evidence which has been studied by and large does not immediately present answers to the above questions. We might say they are not the right questions. For instance, the agendum of inquiry into synagogue remains, which is generated by the evidence itself and not imposed from without, seeks to solve a different set of problems. An example of recent research will illustrate the point. In a doctoral dissertation in Art History, a study of Palestinian synagogue art and architecture, M. J. Chiat assembles a corpus of relevant data. She argues on the basis of this evidence that it is essential to group synagogues for architectural analysis by geopolitical locale within Palestine.[21] Chiat emphasizes the value of associating sites by region rather than by a hypothetical countrywide system of classification. Her compilation shows significant distinction in architectural design from one region to another in various sectors of Palestine. She rejects therefore, on the basis of her study, the formerly prevalent theory of three epochs in Pan-Palestinian synagogue architecture--early, transitional and

late--corresponding to the rise of Palestinian rabbinism
(2nd-3rd centuries), its development (late 3rd through 5th C.),
and its decline (5th-8th C.).[22] She shows, for instance, significant variation in architectural form and decoration in the
territories of Tiberias, Sepphoris, Scythopolis and Tetracomia
in the Northern Sector of Palestine. This concurs well with M.
Smith's observation of first-century Palestine that "the different parts of the country were so different, such gulfs of feeling and practice separated Idumea, Ceasarea and Galilee, that . . .
[with regard to the local religion of the average people] there
was probably no more agreement between them than between any one
of them and a similar area in the Diaspora."[23] Chiat concludes
further regarding the Palestinian synagogue that "There was no
overriding authority, or normative, accepted liturgy, which would
dictate the form this building was to take. Rather it appears
that each (regional) Jewish community tackled the problem individually by drawing on the resources available within their own
immediate area."[24] Variations in architecture confirm the
regional separation of late antique Palestine, she concludes.
Chiat's inquiry proposes, as it should, a solution to an art
historical issue generated by the corpus of evidence which she
seeks to interpret. It may be appropriate to address a secondary set of issues to this data, those questions which I mentioned above about prayer in general. Some might argue that by
extending Chiat's results, for instance, it would be plausible
to assume that prayers recited and the manner of praying in
various Palestinian synagogues varied from locale to locale.
Hence one might conclude that it is unlikely that a unitary
liturgy for first-, second-, or third-century Palestine existed.
The pattern of regional development of design and decoration
could then perhaps be extended to synagogue life in general in
Roman Palestine. Consequently, synagogue remains may provide
information regarding patterns and types of style and decoration
and their development and suggest broader conclusions as well.
The art historical methods used, for instance, in the above study
may indirectly inform us concerning the synagogue's function for
prayer or some other purpose even though these may not be appropriate primary avenues of inquiry for this set of data.

Recent research on diaspora synagogues, however, suggests
that the synagogue evidence may be more exhaustively exploited
for the reconstruction of the function and life of the synagogue.
A. T. Kraabel, in his study of the "Social System of Six Diaspora
Synagogues,"[25] draws inferences from synagogue design about the

social significance of the buildings in their respective settings. More important for our present concerns, he suggests that on the basis of the evidence one may confidently hypothesize what the nature of the liturgic activity inside the structures may have been. He remarks, for example, that from the evidence of "four sites one might assume that scriptures dominate the religious life of the community."[26] Teaching, he further remarks, was an important activity of the synagogue. We can know, moreover, about the functionaries of the institutions including the synagogue staff or officers, priests, and communal leaders.[27] Now these conclusions and observations are, to be sure, general, and they may represent the limits of our knowledge of the function of the ancient synagogue in Judaic life. It remains to be seen whether the results of further sound, conservative, art-historical and archaeological research on the one hand, and the conclusions of critical analysis of literary traditions on the other, will further illumine our understanding of early rabbinic prayer and other related phenomena of nascent rabbinic Judaism.[28]

To this point I have limited my remarks to two sets of data--literary traditions of prayer-texts and archaeological remains of late antique synagogues. Other literary traditions relevant to the study of early rabbinic liturgy include, in particular, traditions in Mishnah, Tosefta, the Talmudim and Midrashim which deal with prayer.[29] The bulk of these materials are legal dicta concerning prayer. Past scholars have viewed these rabbinic legal dicta mainly unidimensionally. They assumed that the most dominant purpose and function of these statements was to regulate the liturgic practice of late antique Jews. The study of these materials was of interest because it indicated the range of actions which Jews performed or were supposed to perform. Naturally those who took this basically positivist view frequently sought to correlate the laws of prayer with the evidences of prayer-texts[30] (most of which is derived from that selfsame literary source of rabbinic traditions) or with material evidences of the period. A respectable example of such an attempt to correlate legal literary traditions with material remains will illustrate the limits of such studies. Y. Yadin's brief monograph, *Tefillin from Qumran* (XQ phyl 1-4), represents such an effort.[31] He examines the remains of the capsule of a head tefillin[32] containing four folded slips. His conclusions show how in many aspects the construction of the capsule and the scribal techniques of the slips of biblical citations reflect "rabbinic traditions" while in some respects the technology of this head tefillin shows divergence from the "Halakhah." Yadin clearly and without justification assumes in this work that rabbinic law served as the sole normative basis for Pan-Judean piety.[33] Yet his study nonetheless shows how the combined mastery of literary and material evidence may lead to fructifying hypotheses and, possibly, open new avenues for further exploration of significant religious phenomena.[34]

To review, material evidences which may be relevant to the context of early Jewish prayer must be subjected to scholarly analysis first by specialists in the methods of archeological and art historical study. I have suggested that the general conclusions of such research about, for instance, the regionality of the decor and design of the synagogues in Roman Palestine may be extended plausibly to all aspects of liturgic activity. Moreover it has been shown that the material evidences of synagogue remains may provide general but direct information concerning some social functions of the structure. Finally, by way of one illustration, I have suggested that caution be employed in any attempt to correlate material relics of ancient Judean prayer with rabbinic legal traditions. Research of the past decade has demonstrated the complex and multifaceted character of rabbinic legal corpora. It is necessary therefore to turn at this point to these materials themselves.

IV

RABBINIC RULES AND REGULATIONS

As I have just indicated, in the past historians have taken rabbinic legal dicta which deal with praying or prayers mainly as statements which indicate either how early rabbinic Jews conducted their liturgical life or the practical ways in which they should have undertaken their rituals of prayer. While it may be legitimate to interpret legal materials in such a way,[35] nonetheless recent scholarship has shown that these legal dicta may serve as a source for our knowledge of early rabbinic metaphysical or philosophical attitudes towards prayer.[36]

This assertion is not self-evident and thus requires some elucidation. Mishnah, the cornerstone of rabbinic legal thought, appears on a superficial reading to be a somewhat stylized and idiosyncratic primitive legal code. Past research, as I suggested above, did little to distinguish the rules and laws of early rabbinic texts from the institutions to which they related. Hence laws of prayer or praying, for instance, were thought of as direct representations of the institution of rabbinic prayer. These rules possessed no independent substantive meaning of their own. Thus it was thought there was little need to study the development of law apart from the development of other social and religious institutions. Such a dichotomy was not clearly recognized or understood. Hence it was not relevant to the scholarly methodology for research into late antique Judaism.[37] Recent anthropological and sociological study of rules of ritual and of law and theoretical jurisprudential studies in general make more precise distinctions and rely on more sophisticated methodological conventions. In particular it has been said by anthropologists that rules for ritual forms conceal complex cognitive apparati.[38] Moreover, it has been asserted by legal historians that laws conceal underlying and unifying general principles and significant sets of ideals governed by reason.[39] Expressed by diverse scholars in a number of ways, a growing consensus of research tends to assert that laws, or rules, must be conceived of, and studied apart from, the institutions which they may potentially regulate. In this regard some see law as an independent "meta-institution" which, in order to regulate society, stands above "other social institutions and modes of customary behavior."[40] On this basis one may further suggest that just as law serves as a meta-institution vis-à-vis other social institutions, so religious law may be seen as a meta-religious realm above and apart from religious institutions of society. The conceptual system of religious law, in other words, hovers above the concrete religious system of a given group--its worldview and way of life. It expresses in a complex fashion a worldview *of* a way of life. In any case, if rules are more than simple extensions of historical and social institutions, we must describe, at least briefly, how laws in rabbinic literature express a meta-system of ideas which relate to our present concerns, the study of early rabbinic prayer.

Again, the nature of the evidence determines the methods of our research. The most extensive and coherent rabbinic sources of information regarding the metaphysics of prayers, early rabbinic concepts of praying, and the meaning of prayer-formulae, are the tractates Berakhot--which deal with prayer--in M., T., B., and Y. Some explicit theological statements and metaphysical assertions concerning prayer appear episodically throughout both this literature and Midrashic compilations. Even so we have no direct sustained equivalent of the explicitly theological and philosophical third-century Christian treatises on prayer written by Origen, Tertullian, or Cyprian.[41] Our most useful sources are the collected legal dicta which indirectly present metaphysical concepts.

In interpreting this data we undertake a three-tiered process. We seek first to describe the ideational structure of the conceptual world of the evidence. We seek next to trace the history of these ideas. Finally, we "ask about the interplay between ideas and social, material reality."[42] I will address presently my program for accomplishing the first two stages of this process and, in the concluding section of this paper (sec. V) I will return to the last stage of the process.

Legal dicta may express philosophical ideas in several ways.[43] We need to decipher the metaphysical import first of individual laws. These may convey significant notions of prayer: e.g., that one must have proper intention while reciting prayers (M. 2:1 for the *shema*`; M. 5:1 for the *tefillah*); that effective formulae of prayer must be fixed or that they may be fluid (M. 1:4 for blessings of the *shema*` and in general; M. 4:3-4 for the *tefillah*-formula). The legal form of each individual statement enhances "the aura of factuality"[44] of each ruling. It may be said that by expressing basic concepts in this way rabbinic authorities enhanced the potential metaphysical or religious impact of each individual legal pericope.

Second, larger conglomerations of laws, such as chapters or tractates of Mishnah, may express more general and extensive theories of prayer. These larger units in M. Berakhot, for instance, illustrate rabbinic notions of how one may conceive of the structure of rituals of the liturgy. Specifically, intermediate divisions of M. outline the major concerns which are integral to such religious actions: i.e., time, composition, intention, distraction, and error (M. 1:1-2:3 for the *shema* and M. 4:1-5:5 for the *tefillah*). The M. tractate Berakhot as a whole conveys the theoretical assertion that what binds diverse rituals of prayer together (*shema*`, *tefillah*, food and meal liturgy, other liturgic occasions) is the focus on the blessing-formulary common to each liturgy. Some smaller units express through detailed rulings larger conceptions about the need for caution in the use of liturgic formulae (M. 5:5, M. 6:4-7). One short conglomerate of rules shows how through the requirements for prayer one may articulate a conception of the structure of the relevant natural world (M. 6:1-3).

One might argue further that on yet another level M.'s laws articulate larger, more general rabbinic philosophic notions. I briefly list a few such conceptions which are suggested by the materials in M. Berakhot: one's will or intention controls his world; one has the ability to rationally understand and control his actions and the structure of his world; one can perceive unity in otherwise chaotic diversity (of ritual-life); words are a source of power which must be unleashed judiciously under controlled conditions; through ritual one may express a natural cosmology.[45]

Once the symbolic, conceptual, and philosophical meaning of individual dicta and of larger legal units which deal with prayer has been described, the next step is to show how these conceptions conform to general rabbinic philosophic attitude expressed through other legal essays in the remaining M. tractates. We wish to know how these ideas fit first into the ideational system of rabbinic thought of M. as a whole,[46] then into other legal conceptual systems in the remaining works of rabbinic literature.

Having established the outlines of the rabbinic metaphysic of prayer, we next seek to trace the historical development of the doctrines and conceptions of prayer which M. Ber., for instance, expresses symbolically in its laws. This enterprise is an exercise in the history of ideas which will show the development of the prominent conceptual concerns of some rabbinic thinkers from the first to the third centuries (C.E.). The aim of this undertaking clearly is not to find the origin of *prayers* or trace the evolution of the liturgy. Nor does it seek to outline real-life synagogue practice over the span of three centuries. But, as I have explained, it aims to demonstrate how some rabbinic statements on the subject of praying and prayers make subtle, symbolic and significant metaphysical statements. It attempts in addition, where possible, to identify how individual creativity affects the course of ideational development. It seeks accordingly to show how ideas of one generation generate further conceptual creativity at later times. The study of rabbinic legal traditions concerning prayer then yields important data for analysis of the third aspect of the general phenomenon of prayer which I referred to at the outset. It will provide information about the metaphysical or philosophical concepts of rabbinic thought expressed through rulings on the procedures for praying and on the prayer-texts and formulae for the prayers themselves.

V
CONCLUSION

It has been said that "the history of a religion is the social relation of the worldview and way of life of that religion to the material reality of the people who held those ideas."[47] Within this general definition I have outlined the preceding theoretical approach to early rabbinic prayer. To review, I have argued that one must frame appropriate questions regarding early Jewish prayer on the basis of available corpora of literary and material data. I have shown that it is necessary to maintain the consideration of distinct aspects of this complex concern with the history of early prayer separate from one another. At the same time I assert that one must recognize the interrelationship of distinct issues which inform the study of *prayer*—the unifying abstract phenomenon at issue.

I have sought to foster throughout a clearer recognition of the interdisciplinary nature of this problem. I have implicitly alluded to some of the potential difficulties of communicating methodological approaches of inquiry and substantive results of research across the diverse disciplinary bounds of philological study, literary criticism, archaeology, art history, history of religions, and the history of law.

I suggest in conclusion that once defined, each aspect of this interdisciplinary problem—history of early Jewish prayer—is amenable to some independent solution. This I have shown briefly, for example, in discussing my research program on the Mishnaic law of prayer. The ways in which solutions to related problems—once achieved—finally may inform one another will not be simple. For the new history of early Jewish prayer will encompass:

(1) A better critical assessment of the early development of the liturgy itself and a new understanding of the limits of our knowledge of this issue.

(2) A more precise understanding of the physical material contexts and objects of prayer in the time of early rabbinic Judaism.

(3) A critical-historical analysis of the rabbinic metaphysic expressed in conceptions of prayer in legal compilations.

The complete picture of the development of this single phenomenon of the history of Judaism will emerge not as a neat, coherent package, the results of which will shape a single integrated narrative description. Rather it will consist of a series of related problems investigated by diverse methods and brought together to address urgent concerns. The problem of defining this phenomenon and its related issues urgently presents itself. The work in each related subdiscipline moves forward. And the opportunities for interdisciplinary cooperation and communication continue to increase. It is now our task to bring into conversation diverse methods for studying the complex data of the past so that we may better know the antecedents of our culture and understand more profoundly the human condition of our own age.

NOTES TO CHAPTER THREE

[1] I do not propose a definition of the phenomenon of prayer in general or of rabbinic prayer in particular here at the outset. Rather I take for granted a shared, intuitive notion of prayer.

[2] By contrast, shared fellowship meals, for instance, may be sacral religious phenomena, or they may be simple occasions of commensality with no symbolic significance.

[3] Most historical accounts of Judaic prayer emphasize this. See, e.g., Ismar Elbogen, *The Historical Development of Prayer in Israel* (Hebrew ed. of the Leipzig 1913 ed.) (Tel Aviv, 1972), and Lawrence A. Hoffman, *The Canonization of the Synagogue Service* (Notre Dame, 1979).

[4] In the third century in particular we find significant evidence of Christian interest in prayer. Cf. the early Christian essays on prayer: Origen, *Treatise on Prayer*; Tertullian, *De Oratione*; Cyprian, *De Oratione*.

[5] See, e.g., M. Ber. 4:4, T. Ber. 3:7, B. Ber. 16b-17a, Y. Ber. 4:2, 7d.

[6] By Amram Gaon (857-871). Cf. Elbogen; E. D. Goldschmidt, *On Jewish Liturgy* (Jerusalem, 1978); J. Heinemann, *Prayer in the Time of the Tannaim and Amoraim* (Jerusalem, 1966; English version: R. Sarason, Berlin, 1977).

[7] Hoffman, *Canonization*, p. 8.

[8] Ibid., p. 4.

[9] Heinemann's form-critical approach appears to reject the basic assumptions of the *Wissenschaft*-philological approach. Instead of assuming a single normative liturgy throughout early rabbinic Judaism he presupposes greater liturgic fluidity. Still he insists that ultimately some Tannaitic authority selects the official texts for worship out of the extant spectrum. A detailed critique of early work on the liturgy appears in R. S. Sarason, "On the Use of Method in the Modern Study of Jewish Liturgy," in *Approaches to Ancient Judaism: Theory and Practice*, ed. W. Green (Missoula, Mont., 1978), pp. 97-172.

[10] By way of contrast see Elbogen, and especially A. Millgram, *Jewish Worship* (Philadelphia, 1971). See M. Brocke's comments on the latter and on numerous studies of the liturgies of synagogue and church in *The Lord's Prayer and Jewish Liturgy*, ed. J. J. Petuchowski and M. Brocke (New York, 1978), pp. 205-20.

[11] See Sarason; Hoffman, pp. 2-4; and n. 9 above.

[12] Cf. L. Finkelstein, "The Development of the Amidah," *JQR* 16 (1925-1926):1-43, 127-70, and "The Birkat Hamazon," *JQR* 19 (1929):211-62; Heinemann; and Sarason, pp. 112-18, 131-49.

[13] Cf. M. Ber. 1:1-3:5, T. Ber. 1:1-10.

[14] Elie Munk, *The World of Prayer*, 2 vols. (New York, 1961-1963), is a fine example of a study of the meaning and import of prayers. Though uncritical and theological in his

approach, Munk, through attention to the details of the liturgy, extracts a wealth of concepts and ideas from the standard prayerbook.

[15] S. C. Heilman, *Synagogue Life* (Chicago, 1976), a somewhat idiosyncratic anthropologically oriented study of American Orthodox synagogue ritual and interaction.

[16] See, e.g., Matt. 6:1-18, 22-25; Luke 18:9-14.

[17] E.g., T. Ber. 1:2, 1:4; M. Ber. 1:3. Also cf. the Qumran Literature, Manual of Discipline (IQSl), Damascus Document (CDC 6), and scattered references in Ben Sirah. For a general summary see C. W. F. Smith, "Prayer," *IDB* (Nashville, 1962) 3:857-67.

[18] The bulk of the relevant evidence rests in rabbinic compilations. The critical work on M. and T. has been done. See J. Neusner, *History of the Mishnaic Law of Purities* (Leiden, 1974-1977), *History of the Mishnaic Law of Holy Things* (Leiden, 1978-1979), *History of the Mishnaic Law of Women* (Leiden, 1979-1980), *History of the Mishnaic Law of Appointed Times* (Leiden, expected in 1981), *History of Mishnaic Law of Damages* (Leiden, expected in 1982), and *Judaism: The Evidence of Mishnah* (Chicago, expected in 1981).

[19] See Section II, above.

[20] See Section IV, below.

[21] M. J. Chiat, *A Corpus of Synagogue Art and Architecture in Roman and Byzantine Palestine* (Ph.D. dissertation, University of Minnesota, 1979).

[22] So Avi-Yonah as cited and discussed by Chiat, pp. 759ff.

[23] M. Smith, "Palestinian Judaism in the First Century," in *Israel: Its Role in Civilization*, ed. Moshe Davis (New York, 1956), p. 81, and cited by Chiat, p. 4.

[24] Ibid., p. 782.

[25] Kraabel's discussion of structures at Sardis, Priene, Dura, Delos, Ostia, and Stobi will appear in *Ancient Synagogues: The Current State of Research. Religion and Art*, 5, ed. J. Guttmann (Missoula, 1980).

[26] Art. cit., see V.

[27] Art. cit., see VI.

[28] Cf. S. Neusner, "The Symbolism of Ancient Judaism: The Evidence of the Synagogues," in Guttmann. An illustration of an early, uncritical attempt at synthesizing a variety of evidences can be found in S. Krauss, *Synagogale Altertümer* (1922; reprint ed., Hildesheim, 1966).

[29] Most appear in tractate Berakhot of M., T., B., and Y.

[30] Cf. Heinemann, Elbogen, and most others including H. L. Strack and P. Billerbeck, *Kommentar Zum Neuen Testament aus Talmud und Midrash* (Munich, 1928).

[31] Y. Yadin, *Tefillin from Qumran* (Jerusalem, 1969).

[32] The assumption that tefillin are to be associated with rituals of praying is a projection back to the first century based on firmer knowledge of later practice. See M. Shabuot 3:8, 3:11 for mention, at least, of a formal rabbinic ritual of wearing tefillin.

[33] Remarks on this supposition may be found in J. Neusner, "The Demise of Normative Judaism," in *Early Rabbinic Judaism* (Leiden, 1975).

[34] See Yadin, pp. 34-35.

[35] I develop this issue in "Do Rabbinic Rules of Ritual Mirror Social Change," a paper presented at the Fourteenth Conference of the International Association of the History of Religions, Winnipeg, Canada, August 1980.

[36] Cf. J. Neusner, *Judaism: The Evidence of Mishnah*, Introduction.

[37] As legal theory predominantly takes up issues of the institutional implementation of legal dicta and of justice and other practical concerns of legal effectiveness, so too the relatively new arena of *Mishpat Ivri* (viz. M. Elon, "Mishpat Ivri," *Encyclopedia Judaica* 12 [Jerusalem, 1972]:109-51) tends away from the search for inherent conceptual symbolic meanings. Traditional Talmud study also, by and large, does not seek unifying philosophical principles, save for the methods of a few such as J. B. Soloveitchik in the tradition of R. Hayyim of Brisk (viz. A. Lichtenstein, "Joseph Soloveitchik," in *Great Jewish Thinkers of the Twentieth Century*, ed. S. Noveck [Washington, D.C., 1969]).

[38] M. Douglas, *Natural Symbols* (New York, 1973) and illustrated from a wide selection of social, scientific, and humanistic thought in *Rules and Meanings* (New York, 1977).

[39] Thurman Arnold, *The Symbols of Government* (New York, 1962), cited in *Law and Society*, ed. Y. Aubert (New York, 1977), pp. 46-51.

[40] See D. Little and S. B. Twiss, *Comparative Religious Ethics* (New York, 1978), pp. 76-78, for a precise theoretical development of the implications of this notion.

[41] See n. 4 above.

[42] Neusner, *Judaism: The Evidence of Mishnah*, Introduction (MS p. 11).

[43] Consistently demonstrated by Neusner in his history of Mishnaic law (see n. 18, above).

[44] On the import of this concept see C. Geertz, "Religion as a Cultural System," in *Anthropological Approaches to the Study of Religion*, ed. M. Banton (London, 1971).

[45] For the sources of these concepts in the Tractate see my forthcoming monograph, *Early Jewish Prayer: The Evidence of Mishnah* (Minneapolis, 1980).

[46] As the work on M.'s law is now just about done (see n. 18), this analysis now may be undertaken.

[47] Neusner, *Judaism* (MS p. 21).

PART TWO

JUDAISM IN MEDIEVAL TIMES

CHAPTER FOUR

SOME REMARKS ON THE STUDY OF JEWISH PHILOSOPHY IN THE MIDDLE AGES

Aviezer Ravitzky
Hebrew University

I

A student of Jewish philosophy, speaking to an audience of historians dealing with other areas of Jewish activity, is aware that Jewish philosophy has had a limited impact upon Jewish history. To be sure, philosophical or theological literature does not have the same status in the history of Jewish religion and of the Jewish people as does rabbinical-halachic literature, both in the domain of the Jew's daily life and in the domain of the Jew's intellectual enterprise and spiritual creativity. It is true that quite often a philosopher was also a central rabbinical authority and public figure, but this only emphasizes the fact that his main influence, the grounds of his authority for his own generation and for generations to come were his status as a rabbi, as a *posek* or a teacher of halachah, rather than as a philosopher. Neither does the student of Jewish philosophy pretend, on the other hand, that Jewish philosophy had a profound influence under the surface, so to speak, as a vital yet hidden, subterranean current whose historical impact should be recovered, as prominent scholars assert is the case with the kabbala. Jewish philosophy did not create significant movements external to its own history. The failure of the attempt to formulate Jewish dogma, universally accepted principles of faith which serve as the basis of Jewish theology, that failure, too, stands out against the success of halachic codification and to some extent also against the success of the kabbala to provide its basic text with the aura of ancient authority. If all this is so, the historian would ask the student of philosophy, what is the real weight of the philosophical enterprise within the history of Israel and the religion of Israel?

This is not the only direction from which queries are thrust at the student of Jewish philosophy. For example, he is challenged by students of philosophy as such, not in the Jewish context, with a question of a different kind. He is not asked

about the influence or significance of Jewish philosophers such
as Philo or Maimonides (or Spinoza?) within the context of
Western philosophy. But rather: Does Jewish philosophy define
a specific domain within philosophy as such? Can it be defined
by specific teachings common to its own thinkers, or by a clear
and continuous internal tradition? For philosophy, by definition,
by dealing with abstract concepts, with rational modes of argument, and by the character of its questions is universal. And
indeed, even the various schools of Jewish philosophy are characterized according to the schools prevailing in philosophy-at-large, so to speak: Kalamic, Neoplatonic, Aristotelian, Neo-kantian, etc. In the words of Julius Guttmann:

> The history of Jewish philosophy is a history of the
> successive absorptions of foreign ideas which were then
> transformed and adopted according to specific Jewish
> points of view.[1]

Does Jewish philosophy, then, have a well-defined domain of its
own?

The various answers which scholars may come up with to
these questions may reflect not only differences in information
and methodology, but also differences in ideology. Methodologically speaking, however, I propose the following formulation:
even if we avoid the question of the existence of common teaching or of a continuous internal tradition, we may nevertheless
propose a specific framework to the history of Jewish philosophy.
It is a philosophy which deals with a certain <u>problem</u> (or more
precisely, with a certain type of problem), namely the confrontation or encounter of the nonphilosophic Jewish sources and the
non-Jewish philosophic sources.[2] That is, it deals with the
problem of the existence of the Jew as a Jew confronted by his
universal philosophic knowledge and consciousness.[3] As long as
the Jew remains within his own domain, within his religious rabbinic tradition,[4] he does not attempt to construct a philosophy
which has recourse to universal-rational concepts and arguments.
The internal certainty of his particular tradition is sufficient
for him. Whenever, on the other hand, the Jew becomes exposed
to the outside world and its philosophy, such as was the case
in ancient Alexandria, in medieval Spain or in modern Germany,
he constructs a philosophy. Even if the various solutions to
the problem of confrontation are not uniform, even if they do
not reveal continuity, it is the common problem which defines
the domain of Jewish philosophy.

This minimalistic characterization enables us to relate
at the outset to both the query of the historian of Judaism as

to the significance of the philosophic enterprise in the life of
Israel, and the query of the historian of philosophy as to the
specific characteristics of *Jewish* philosophy.

The historian of Judaism will be told that the very
characterization of philosophy as the domain *par excellence* in
which the Jew confronts an alien world of thought establishes
for philosophy a special place in the history of the Jewish
people and of Judaism. It is in this reflective plane that the
Jews thought out for themselves the relationship between their
particularity and their universality, or else formulated their
particularity in universal terms. Thus it has significance
even beyond the domain of philosophy itself. To understand that
significance one should examine not only the subject matter of
philosophy, i.e., the intellectual content of the reaction to
the confrontation itself. One should also examine the scope or
extent of the philosophic enterprise. Was the philosophic
enterprise always the domain of the few, an enterprise whose
legitimacy is always called into question, always alien, or did
this enterprise sometimes penetrate the synagogue, the *yeshiva*,
the curriculum? For example, finding a philosophic sermon given
in a synagogue by the rabbi of the community, and analyzing its
content and sources, is relevant even beyond the domain of the
history of ideas, and is significant even beyond the history of
philosophy itself.

This characterization of Jewish philosophy as philosophy
which arises from a problem, that of the confrontation or encounter between Judaism and philosophy, makes it possible for us to
clarify our approach also to our other colleague, the historian
of philosophy. This colleague knows that one of the contemporary
theories in the historiography of philosophy recommends that the
scholar concentrate on the philosopher's *problems*, those questions
which he attempts to answer, and not on *solutions* or systems
alone. This theory calls upon the scholar to try to uncover the
problems which guided the philosopher in his investigation and in
his conclusions. In the words of John Passmore: "The first
question the problematic historian will ask himself about any
philosopher is: What problem was he trying to solve?"[5] Such a
historian will also try to show that side by side with episodic
or transitional problems there are always recurring problems in
the history of philosophy. For example, he can concentrate on
the history of problems which arise from the confrontation of
the individual and the state, although he is aware of the profound differences between the Greek *polis*, the state of Hobbes,

and the modern liberal state. He will try to uncover recurring problems and understand their development and their transformations.

The analogy between the approach to the history of philosophy in the context of its problems and approaching Jewish philosophy as a discussion of a problem or group of problems may not be all-inclusive, but I believe it is fruitful. In Jewish philosophy, too, there is a certain type of problem, in spite of the fact that in different periods Jewish philosophers confronted different doctrines, and that Aristotelianism and Kantianism do not present an identical set of problems. There is a common material basis to all philosophic doctrines which Judaism confronted, even beyond their existential characterization as representing at all times the "outside," the external world of the Jew. All of these doctrines together can be viewed as an embodiment of the rational, the conceptual, the autonomous, the universal.[6] All of them may be seen in many ways as representative of a tradition, the tradition of philosophy, which Whitehead once described as a series of footnotes on Plato,[7] or as many medieval philosophers would have put it, a series of footnotes on Aristotle. (It was not only philosophy which had undergone transformations. So did the way in which Jews conceived of their own tradition, which was continuously growing; in the matter of Jewish tradition, however, there is no need to demonstrate its continuity.) In a way, one may claim that the problem which motivates the rise of Jewish philosophy is the encounter of two *traditions*, the Jewish tradition and the philosophic tradition.[8]

Methodologically speaking, this approach entails a certain way of viewing the sources of Jewish philosophy. I intend to limit what I say to medieval Jewish philosophy.

One may characterize this way of viewing Jewish philosophy as a sort of possible tension between scholar and text. The scholar tries to uncover the problems from which the text arises as well as those which are inherent in it. As a historian of philosophy he will of course be concerned with every philosophic problem which the author posits. As a historian of Jewish philosophy he will be primarily concerned with those problems which the confrontation of Jewish sources and alien sources brings about. He will try to expose this duality to uncover the gulf between the two worlds in which the philosopher finds himself, and to emphasize the problem which guides the development of a certain system, and which is inherent in it. But the original philosopher's interest might be the very opposite: it is often his aim to attempt to deny the presence of a problem or to represent it as a pseudo-problem. He attempts to reconstruct these two worlds as one world.

If the Jewish philosopher is an Aristotelian, he might claim with Maimonides that the basic Aristotelian teachings are the true and internal teachings of the Law, true and internal teachings which have been lost to the Jews in the course of their exile. It is, as he puts it, not a confrontation but a rediscovery of a glorious truth. If it is Plato who is our philosopher's great authority, then he will claim that Plato learned what he knew from our ancient sages. That is what Judah Abravanel asserted during the Renaissance. It is not a confrontation but a harmonious doctrine arising from a single source. If our writer is an "antiphilosophic" philosopher, as Halevi was, he will certainly try to deny the problem and attempt to construct his religious world as one world, exclusive to the people of Israel, in which no Greek philosopher has a position.

But I would like to emphasize: it is not the scholar who forces upon the text the problem of confrontation with alien philosophic teachings in order to fit the text into an a priori framework which he had worked out for Jewish philosophy. The medieval text itself frequently explicitly states this problem as one of the origins of its discussion. However, the tension between the scholar and the text comes into being and is reflected in the fact that the scholar may uncover this problem even beyond the text's point of origin. He may emphasize the problem inherent in the solutions themselves, in the system or outcome of a dialogue, or in the conclusion itself. For example, the scholar may find that the tension between the concept of free Divine Will and the concept of Divine Wisdom in the teaching of Maimonides embodies the conflict between the God of creation and the Aristotelian God, which cognizes itself, at the very center of Maimonides' doctrine and not only in the outset of his teaching. The corrolaries and further transformations of this internal problem in Maimonides' theology may be uncovered by the scholar in the writings of Maimonideans throughout the thirteenth century as well.[9] Thus the scholar is concerned not only in the way the confrontation is reflected in the problems which give rise to a philosophic composition but also in the way it is reflected in the problems embodied in the content of the composition itself, in its purported solutions, and even in the problems engendered by the text in the writings of others. Hence the scholar should have a critical orientation toward the text,

an orientation which will lead him to be concerned also with
what is not said in the text, or with what is not said explicitly.
Perhaps the scholar is thus reaching beyond the formulations of
the theory of "problematic history." One may also raise the
objection that an orientation of this kind willy-nilly reflects
the scholar's personal point of view as to the continuous and
insoluble character of the problem of confrontation, in all its
manifestations. However: Is it possible to write a history of
a philosophy without any notion about the character of this
philosophy,[10] and thus to engage in apathetic doxography? To be
sure, the scholar must show that what he has to say is firmly
footed in the text and its interpretation.[11]

II

The methodological question is not only a question of the
scholar's orientation towards the philosophical content, but also
the question of selectivity and scope of the texts being investigated. I would like to make a few remarks about this problem,
and then to try to tie them to the general conception proposed
above.

Until recent times most scholarship in Jewish philosophy
concentrated, for obvious reasons, on those writings which were
in book form. These included the writings of the most important
Jewish philosophers as well as other books which were published
especially during the period of *Wissenschaft des Judentums* in
accordance with manuscripts then available and perhaps also
according to the tastes of the publishers. Thus the provenance
of manuscripts in European libraries and the accidental or pro-
fessional considerations of publishers had a decisive influence
in determining the scope of research in medieval Jewish philosophy. In recent years scholarship has turned anew to writings
still in manuscript, and one can already say that a good many
chapters in the history of Jewish philosophy will have to be
rewritten in the light of all available literature. Examples of
possible accidental distortions in a history which takes into
account only printed books abound. I will cite a few instances
from a single area--Jewish philosophy in the thirteenth century.
The philosophic encyclopedia *Sha'ar Hashamayim* by Gershon ben
Shlomo was printed, perhaps as a result of a publisher's mistaken
identification, as a work of Gershon, the father of Gersonides.
Scholarship, though, at least took cognizance of *Sha'ar Hashamayim*. But it remained ignorant of Yehuda ben Shlomo Hacohen's
most interesting encyclopedia, *Midrash Hokhmah*,[12] and of Shem-Tov

Falaquera's comprehensive encyclopedia, "De'ot Hapilosofim." Another example: Scholarship took cognizance of the fourteenth/ fifteenth-century commentaries on Maimonides' *Guide*, but the earlier commentaries, those of Moses of Salerno[13] and Zeraḥyah Ḥen[14] of the thirteenth century, were not even included in an edition of commentaries called *Qadmone Mefarshe Hamore*, "The Earliest Commentators of the *Guide*." Scholarship ignored them. Samuel Ibn Tibbon's *Ma'amar Yiqavu Hamayim* was published, but his philosophical commentary on Ecclesiastes, which is indispensable for the understanding of his philosophy, is still in manuscript. The same fate is enjoyed by the work of Samuel's son, Moses Ibn Tibbon, whose commentary on the Song of Songs is in print, but his commentary on the *aggadot* of the sages, *Sefer Pe'ah*, which is the one book in which his distinctive point of view comes out clearly, is still unpublished. A final example: The book *Livyat Ḥen*, by the persecuted philosopher Levi ben Abraham, who symbolizes for the opponents of philosophy in the controversy of 1303 the very dangerous character of philosophy, is still in manuscript. In the light of these and other facts we are justified in saying that the history of Jewish philosophy in the thirteenth century, which saw the great controversy over Maimonides' writings and over the legitimacy of philosophy, has not yet been written. Below, I will mention another example relating to another period in the history of Jewish philosophy. At any rate it seems clear that the study of manuscripts will yield many surprises and new perspectives, which are not necessarily related to a specific approach toward the history of Jewish philosophy but simply to the furthering of our knowledge and to extending the material which is available to the scholar.

Nevertheless, this is not only a question of accruing information but one of orientation toward the kind of text that should be sought. I will now discuss two aspects of this question.

1. *Disciples and Interpretation*

The primary consideration which moves a scholar to study a certain philosophical text is its intrinsic significance, its standard of argumentation, its originality, the profundity of its interpretation of Jewish sources, and the like. Such considerations are what have made scholars select Crescas' *Or Hashem* as a focus of research in preference to his disciple Albo's *Sefer Haiqqarim*, in spite of the fact that the later book has attained a far greater popularity throughout the ages. Scholarship preferred the philosophical criterion over the historical criterion of sociocultural impact. This, however, is not a result of the discovery of new manuscripts, but rather of a different perspective, a different evaluation of well-known texts. The study of the writings of the most important philosophers is not, as a rule, based upon the study of manuscripts. (We are not discussing the preparation of scientific editions.) To be sure, even when we deal with a philosopher of the rank of Crescas, a scholar may discover a forgotten manuscript of his which has gathered dust in two libraries as a result of faulty evaluation by two nineteenth-century scholars.[15] Yet, this is not the usual case, and the writings of the most important philosophers were published in several editions.

Yet there is another consideration, which is not connected to the identification of the writings of these philosophers, but is relevant to the study of their teachings. One may speak about a certain philosophical teaching not only by analyzing its fundamental or original text but by studying its progressive articulation in the writings of disciples, of its progressive reconstruction in the generations which followed. As L. Tatarkiewicz put it:

> A complete history of philosophy must be in part the history of individuals and in part that of groups . . . the history of philosophy is in part the history of the formation of philosophical ideas and in part the history of their diffusion.[16]

From that perspective there is a special significance to the study of manuscripts. The processes of partial adaption and partial transformation of ideas, of their development in the writings of semidisciples and semiredactors, of wrestling with problems inherent in the fundamental, original source—all this cannot of course be culled from the printed texts of the great philosophers themselves. If the history of philosophy also includes these processes, one needs to reexamine the development and fate of philosophical teachings in Jewry.

What significance would this reexamination have? Is it relevant to the interpretation of these teachings themselves?

Our answer to this question depends first of all on our general approach to the problem of interpretation. What kind of texts can an interpretation use in addition to the very texts which contain the interpreted teaching? Does interpretation take into its purview only the sources of a teaching, trying to rethink it in the light of the sources, or should an interpretation also take into account different types of texts, namely those which were developed in response to, were influenced by, or were critical of the teaching and revealed new ways of reading it?

For when we assert that a certain text was influenced by another, or that a certain concept is based on another one, we are not only interpreting the latter text or idea, but in a way we are interpreting the original source as well. We learn about various logical possibilities inherent in it, we learn about the ways it anticipates development in various directions. When Spinoza said, for example, that when "certain Jews" spoke about the unity of God with His intelligibilia, they "felt as if through the fog"[17] a central concept in his--Spinoza's--teaching, does this not inform us about an inherent problem, about dynamite concealed in the teachings of Jewish Aristotelians such as Maimonides? Or when Gilson[18] claimed that there is a strong connection between the philosophy of Descartes and medieval philosophy, or when Wolfson[19] claimed the same about Spinoza and medieval philosophy, do we learn from those assertions only about modern philosophy or also about medieval philosophy?

This has to do with the problem of interpretation as such. As to the special character of Jewish philosophy, it is even more significant: if Jewish philosophy is concerned primarily with the problem of confrontation or encounter of Judaism and philosophy, if our intention is to examine whether this problem appears only at the outset or also in the proposed solution, if there is a so-called tension between the scholar and the author whenever the scholar attempts to recover the unreconciled gaps between the philosopher's two worlds, then we need to learn how disciples wrestled with our philosopher's teachings, to clarify the text's problems as seen[20] by both followers and critics. The dynamic view of the history of Jewish philosophy in its various transformations makes an investigation of this nature all-important.

2. *The Range of the Philosophic Enterprise*

The question of the influence of a philosopher over circles of disciples, the question of how his teaching was expounded both orally and in writing, is significant not only for understanding his philosophy as such but also for learning about the range or actual status of the philosophic enterprise in Jewish history. We have discussed the problem of school, discipleship, and articulation of a teaching having in mind the teaching itself and its interpretation. But the use of the vast literature still in manuscript not only aids the study of the history of philosophy but also helps clarify the general historical problem: Was the philosophic enterprise always only the portion of the few, or did it also penetrate the synagogue, the *yeshiva*, and the public at large?

According to many philosophers, philosophy is by definition a domain of the few, and is an activity which reflects an exclusive dimension in an individual's life, that same aspect whereby he is differentiated from his community. This plane of existence, his philosophic activity, has only individual and universal dimensions, but no communal one. That is of course not to say that the philosopher is necessarily oblivious to the socio-political aspect of mankind, that every philosopher is necessarily an advocate of the solitary way of life. It may mean, for example, that in order to communicate successfully he does not use the intellectual-philosophical function of the soul but other functions, such as the imaginative one. Moreover, as a philosopher he has only an intellectual biography, which he is willing to share with "the one who is superior," and not with "ten thousand fools."[21] This approach is revealed in all its acuity in the view of several philosophers about the esoteric character of philosophy. Not only do the masses not react positively to philosophy and it finds its way only to the few, but it ought not be widely disseminated, and thus it is incumbent upon the philosopher to conceal his views from the many. To illustrate this I would like to mention what Samuel Ibn Tibbon says in his commentary on Ecclesiastes. He describes how the Jewish communities of the early thirteenth century were divided into an anti-Maimonidean majority and a small Maimonidean minority, a very tiny minority. Ibn Tibbon asserts provocatively that even these few supporters of Maimonides did not understand him properly. Had they known what Maimonides was really up to, they would have joined the camp of his opponents.[22] This of course is an extreme position which is not necessarily shared by everyone, but it illustrates an individualistic and esoteric view of philosophy which does not compromise even for the sake of "public relations" and does not leave room for the dissemination of philosophy among the many.

If this is the case, why did Ibn Tibbon translate the *Guide* into Hebrew, thereby enlarging its audience very greatly, and why did he append to his translation a philosophical glossary whose intention was to explain standard philosophical terms to a reader who is untrained in philosophy? How are we to explain the fact that his student and son-in-law Jacob Anatoli delivered philosophical sermons in the synagogue, while being at the same time faithful to his teacher's esoteric conception of philosophy, to which conception he paradoxically alluded in his public sermons? The fate of Anatoli's sermons shows well the insoluble tension between the need to conceal and the need to disseminate: he was compelled to cease speaking in public under the pressure, in his own words, of "some of my friends,"[23] and we have no way of knowing whether these were the opponents of philosophy or philosopher-colleagues who were opposed to the popularizing of philosophy. At any rate, two generations later his sermons were returned to the synagogue. Anatoli's descendants read them in public in protest against the opponents of philosophy in their own time and place.[24] These examples illustrate the situation in the post-Maimonidean era but they clearly exemplify the problematic place of philosophical enterprise among the many, from both the point of view of the philosopher and the reaction of the public. Many chapters in the history of this problem have as yet not been explored; they are still in manuscript. The uncovering of these chapters would be helpful also in perceiving Jewish philosophy as a history of the confrontation or encounter of Judaism and philosophy, from the point of view not only of philosophical content but of the awareness of those dealing with philosophy. We can find it, for example, in the philosophic commentaries on the Bible and the post-biblical literature who wrestle with every verse and every Midrash in the attempt to harmonize the two worlds, often forcing the text to fit it into their mold; in the Hebrew philosophic encyclopedias meant to be widely disseminated, or in philosophic correspondence, or in notes prepared for lectures, or in philosophic sermons, and even in introductions to Hebrew translations of Greek or Arabic philosophic texts which describe their intention to give philosophy back to the Jew, who is its true source. In this sense the post-Maimonidean era brings out more sharply perhaps than other periods the general problem or topic of Jewish philosophy--the confrontation of Judaism and philosophy and sometimes also the confrontation of the one and the many.

III

Are the methods outlined above fruitful? In the main, do we have a philosophical literature upon which their efficacy could be tested? Namely, do we have disciples' texts in which a philosophical teaching was implanted? I will try to illustrate briefly the approaches mentioned above with the two outstanding medieval Jewish philosophers--Maimonides and Crescas. Most of my work has heretofore been devoted to these philosophers and their disciples. Philosophical teachings and the history of the problem of confrontation cannot unfortunately be covered in this paper, but a brief review of the historical and textual framework will suffice.

1. *Maimonides*

Maimonides' influence on Jewish philosophy is more significant than that of any other medieval philosopher, and Jewish medieval philosophy following Maimonides has recourse mainly to his philosophy. It either agrees with Maimonides or is critical of him. *The Guide of the Perplexed* determines in a certain way the philosophical concerns of later philosophy at least to the end of the fifteenth century. This is well known and has been noted by many scholars.

It is thus the more remarkable that, to begin with, our knowledge of the earlier commentators of the *Guide* and of the immediate dissemination of its teaching is very limited. Serious philosophical discussion of its teaching is generally assigned by scholars to the fourteenth and fifteenth centuries. Furthermore, scholarship has not yet traced the growth of a continuous school, which developed through a gradual elaboration of the issues, and in which every thinker relates to the teachings of Maimonides through the preceding interpretations.

The examination of thirteenth-century philosophical literature, which is in manuscript, leads us to amend the previously held incomplete historical view. First, manuscript research informs us about Maimonidean exegesis and the discussion of his teaching in the century immediately following him. Second, it uncovers for the first time the existence of a continuous school, which interprets the *Guide* both directly and indirectly through the thirteenth century. All of this permits us to reconstruct the origins of the most comprehensive and most interesting development in the history of Jewish philosophy, the history of the *Guide* and its adventures through the ages.

Some of these thinkers have been mentioned above. The tradition I am describing begins with the writings of Samuel Ibn Tibbon, continues with Jacob Anatoli and Moses Ibn Tibbon, and is passed by Anatolio the son of Jacob Anatoli to Moses of Salerno, the author of the first sentence-by-sentence commentary on the *Guide*. The tradition continues through Isaiah the son of Moses of Salerno, and thereafter the powerful influence of the Tibbonides is apparent in the writings of Zerahyah Hen and his disciples in Rome, and in the activity of the descendants of the Tibbonides, Jacob ben Makir, and Judah Ibn Tibbon in the Provence, toward the end of the thirteenth and the beginning of the fourteenth century. It is interesting to note that in most cases these writers were themselves conscious of the continuity of their philosophical tradition.

For these thinkers the philosophy of Maimonides became the official philosophy of Judaism, and indeed we find someone who says it cannot be contradicted even by recourse to the authority of *Ḥazal*--the sages![25] A twofold attitude towards the *Guide* is developed. On the one hand it is an esoteric text whose author abjured his readers not to reveal its secret teachings; on the other hand it is a book whose teaching should become the authentic interpretation of Judaism. An exclusive text, but one that must influence and educate the youth. The *Guide* will come to be taught on two levels, for two kinds of readers. Eventually we witness a so-called paradox of a public sermon including esoteric teaching.

From the point of view of the character of Jewish philosophy as a confrontation or an encounter between Judaism and philosophy, one should keep in mind that the thinkers we are discussing are at the same time the translators of Greek and Arabic philosophy into Hebrew. Their activity determines to a great extent what foreign writings and teachings will be brought to the attention of the Hebrew reader. They are also philosophical commentators of the Bible and of post-biblical literature, and this activity too is an expression of the confrontation of the Jewish source and the philosophic doctrine, the attempt to "Judaize" philosophy while searching for philosophic content in the Bible and in the Midrash. The attempt to harmonize Judaism and philosophy becomes a daily activity, concretely expressed in their wrestling with every biblical verse, every *midrash*, every *aggadah*. At the same time they are clearly aware of the philosophic accomplishments of their Christian environment, and call explicitly for parallel dissemination of philosophy in Jewish circles.

As to the status of the philosophic enterprise, it is important to emphasize that these thinkers assert only their philosophic competence and are not claimants to rabbinical authority. They are not halachists. The philosopher is sometimes in conflict with rabbinical figures, but sometimes acts in concert with a rabbi or a head of a *yeshiva*, who recognizes his place as the representative of Maimonidean teaching and of the *ḥokhmot ḥizzoniyot*, the foreign sciences. A good example is the

attitude of Jonathan Hacohen of Lunel to Samuel Ibn Tibbon. In
addition, one should note that those philosophers were not isolated cases, but often influential teachers who were in the midst
of a philosophic circle. They constantly refer in their writings
to their colleagues and to their students, and some of their
writings were composed as a result of public lectures or sermons.

The investigation of the earliest reception of Maimonides'
teaching among these disciples is important not only historically
but also philosophically. Much can be learned from their philosophical analysis and interpretation, but I can not deal with
this matter here.[26] I would, however, like to note that continuity of tradition does not necessarily mean identity of view.
Among the earliest interpreters of Maimonides, one can already
discern the beginnings of the two alternative approaches to the
interpretation of Maimonides, alternative approaches which have
continued up to contemporary Maimonidean scholarship. Any history of the influence and development of Maimonides' philosophy
throughout the ages which neglects its origin in the immediate
post-Maimonidean era is clearly defective.

2. *Crescas*

What we know about Crescas' teaching is based almost completely on the book he wrote in the last part of his life, *Or
Hashem*, and on his anti-Christian polemic. Information about
Crescas' philosophy and its interpretation in the writings of his
disciples was until recently very meager. Studies of Crescas
noted a disproportion between his slight imprint on Jewish philosophy and the contemporary reevaluation of the intrinsic significance of his philosophy. Scholars wondered why Crescas had
apparently not left his mark on his contemporaries, save for one
solitary disciple, Joseph Albo.

In the light of the paucity of his writings and the presumed lack of disciples, every additional piece of information
about his teaching and his students becomes all-important. Such
additional information is available to us in manuscript.

To begin with, we find a forgotten writing of Crescas
apparently based on a philosophic sermon which he delivered
before Passover in Saragossa, where he occupied the seat of the
rabbinate. We gain further insight into Crescas' teaching from
this composition. Its complex philosophical content and its
scholastic, brief, and difficult style characteristic of Crescas
make us wonder about the sort of audience and community for which
such a sermon was considered appropriate. Furthermore, it appears

that there was a circle of disciples of Crescas who delivered sermons in the style of their master or composed philosophical compositions from which we can learn about heretofore unknown philosophical doctrines of Crescas. Notable among these disciples is Zeraḥyah Halevi, Crescas' follower in the Saragossa rabbinate, who, while his master was still alive, delivered philosophical sermons in which he publicly took issue with various aspects of his master's teaching. Another disciple, Matityahu Hayitzhari, also adds to our knowledge of unknown teachings of Crescas. Another writer, Joseph ben David, delivered a sermon before Passover and inserted into it long portions of Crescas' Passover sermon, but in the end dissented from his master's consistent philosophic conclusion. Yet another disciple, Abraham bar Leon, apparently wrote his philosophic writing in Crescas' own home somewhat earlier.[27]

Thus we learn about an extensive philosophic enterprise among a community of halachic scholars inspired by Crescas. The study of their writings will make possible for the first time a study of Crescas' teaching in the light of the teachings of his contemporaries and disciples.[28] These manuscripts will also increase our knowledge of the confrontation with the alien world. For example, we will learn about Crescas' relationship to Christian scholastics, e.g., in connection with his unique view denying free will in the matter of faith. Likewise, we will uncover unknown anti-Christian polemics, e.g., in connection with his view of exile and redemption.

* * *

To avoid misunderstanding I would like to end with the following comment. I take strong issue with an approach to the history of philosophy which reduces it to the study of the historical and cultural circumstances of the philosopher or one which reduces philosophy to intellectual history. I do not claim that the student of the history of philosophy should view philosophy as disjointed from all other human activities, but I do believe that the substance of a philosophy must be culled from its internal logic and textual context, not as a function or corollary of other phenomena. Our attempt to follow the development of a school is not designed to provide us simply with a reconstruction of a certain cultural climate, but with greater insight into the construction and transformation of a significant philosophical or theological teaching. Our endeavor to uncover unsystematic philosophical writing, such as biblical commentaries and sermons or epistles, is also directed toward these works' conceptual and rational content; yet it is the primary task of the scholar to uncover the general philosophic doctrines which underlie them. The perception of Jewish philosophy as a framework for the confrontation of Judaism and philosophy indeed presents Jewish philosophy against a backdrop of historical, cultural, or religious encounters, but its main concern is the philosophic ideas born of these encounters.

NOTES TO CHAPTER FOUR

[1] J. Guttmann, *The Philosophy of Judaism* (Philadelphia: Jewish Publication Society, 1964), p. 3. Cf. also S. Pines, "Scholaticism after Thomas Aquinas and the Teaching of Ḥasday Crescas and his Predecessors," *Proceedings of the Israel Academy of Science and Humanities*, 1(10), pp. 1-3; A. Schwied, "Is There an Independent Tradition of Jewish Philosophy" [in Hebrew], in *Ta'am va-Haqasha* (Ramat Gan: Massada, 1970), pp. 12-36; J. Levinger, G. B. Sermonetta and S. Rosenberg, "What is Jewish Philosophy" [in Hebrew], in *Hitgalut, Emunah, Tevunah* (Ramat Gan: Bar Ilan University, 1976), pp. 147-61.

[2] Sometimes the confrontation exists between nonphilosophic Jewish sources and philosophic Jewish sources, the latter serving as moderators of alien philosophy. The confrontation exists sometimes also between Judaism and another religion, rather than between Judaism and philosophy, but when as a result a Jewish philosophy is formed it involves as a rule a philosophic interpretation of the other religion, with which there is a philosophic dispute.

[3] See Levinger, Sermonetta, and Rosenberg, "What is Jewish Philosophy," p. 160.

[4] Or possibly in the Karaite tradition.

[5] J. Passmore, "The Idea of a History of Philosophy," *History and Theory*, Beiheft 5 (1965):1-32, esp. 12-13, 27-32.

[6] Although the confrontation in question takes place between philosophy and an historical phenomenon external to philosophy, e.g., Jewish tradition, it can engender philosophical creativity. Philosophy's encounters with a political community or with another field of knowledge, etc. can also engender philosophical creativity.

[7] A. N. Whitehead, *Process and Reality* (New York, 1969), p. 53. See also H. A. Wolfson, "Extradeical and Intradeical Interpretations of Platonic Ideas," *Journal of the History of Ideas* 22 (1961):31-32.

[8] See S. H. Bergmann, *Toldot Hapilosofia Hahadasha* (Jerusalem: Mosad Bialik, 1970), vol. 1, p. 21.

[9] See A. Ravitzky, "The Hypostasis of the Divine Wisdom in Thirteenth-Century Jewish Thought in Italy: A Neoplatonic Reaction to a Theological Problem" [in Hebrew], *Italia* 4 (1980).

[10] Cf. Zeller's interesting remarks on this subject quoted in H. R. Smart, *Philosophy and Its History* (LaSalle, Ill.: Open Court Publishing Co., 1962), p. 20.

[11] This tension may be viewed from yet another angle. In the study of modern philosophy there is often a tension between the historian of philosophy and the philosopher he studies. The philosopher claims originality, and asserts that there is a great gulf between his philosophy and that of his predecessors, whereas the scholar tries to uncover sources and implant the new system within a continuous tradition. "The occupational disease of the philosopher is to exaggerate his own originality, the occupational disease of the historian is to insist too strongly on continuities" (Passmore, p. 3). However, in medieval philosophy the historian and the philosopher often switch their positions: the

medieval philosopher often claims lack of originality and traditionalism, whereas the historian tries to uncover the philosopher's divergence from his asserted source. The philosopher might represent himself as a commentator, who merely recovers old truths found in either revealed texts or ancient philosophic texts. He might represent himself as one who proposes an interpretation, articulation, or verification of a certain tradition, whereas the historian might point to some development which took place within a religious tradition, or to a religious transformation which an Aristotelian concept underwent, a new development which took place consciously or unconsciously.

[12] See C. Sirat, "Juda B. Salomon Ha-Cohen: philosophe, astronome et peut-être kabbaliste de la première moitié du XIII siècle," *Italia* 2 (1979):39-61.

[13] See G. B. Sermonetta, "The Remarks of Moses of Salerno on the *Guide of the Perplexed*" [in Hebrew], *Iyyun* 20 (1970):212-40.

[14] See n. 9, above, and n. 26, below.

[15] See A. Ravitzky, "A Forgotten Writing of Ḥasday Crescas" [in Hebrew], *Kiryat Sepher* 51 (1976):705-11.

[16] L. Tatarkiewicz, "The History of Philosophy and the Art of Writing It," *Diogenes* 20 (1957):63.

[17] See *Ethics* II, 7, note. See also S. H. Bergmann, *The Philosophy of Salomon Maimon* [in Hebrew] (Jerusalem: Hebrew University, 1932), p. 25.

[18] E. Gilson, *La Liberté chez Descartes et la théologie* (Paris: F. Alcan, 1913).

[19] H. A. Wolfson, *The Philosophy of Spinoza* (Cambridge: Harvard University Press, 1934).

[20] Cf. R. Palmer, *Hermeneutics* (Evanston: Northwestern University Press, 1969), p. 250.

[21] Maimonides, *The Guide of the Perplexed*, Introduction.

[22] Ms. Heb. Parma 272, f. 7-8.

[23] See *Malmad Hatalmidim* (Lyck, 1866), Introduction, p. 12.

[24] See Alba Mari b. Joseph Hayarḥi, *Minḥat Kenaot* (Pressburg, 1838), p. 39.

[25] See Zeraḥyah Ḥen's Epistle to Hillel b. Samuel in *Otsar Neḥmad* 2 (1857):129.

[26] See A. Ravitzky, "The Possibility of Existence and Its Accidentality in Thirteenth-Century Maimonidean Interpretation" [in Hebrew], *Daʿat* 2-3 (1978-79):67-97; idem, "Samuel Ibn Tibbon and the Esoteric Character of the *Guide of the Perplexed*," *AJS Review* 6 (1981) (in press); "Thirteenth-Century Hebrew Quotations from the Lost Arabic Recension of *Parva Naturalia*," *Jerusalem Studies in Arabic and Islam* 3 (1980).

[27] My attention was drawn to this writing by S. Rosenberg in his paper to the Sixth World Congress for Jewish Studies.

[28] One should of course not neglect to mention Joseph Albo and perhaps paragraphs in the writings of Efodi (Profiat Duran).

CHAPTER FIVE

ON STUDYING PHILOSOPHIC MYSTICISM

David Blumenthal
Emory University

For Rafi Zaiman, in memoriam.

I

I would like, in the course of the next few years, to articulate carefully one type of medieval Jewish spirituality: philosophic mysticism.

Before outlining the nature of this expression of Jewish religious sensitivity--its beginnings and its variations--I should like to explain why this subject interests me. This explanation in effect reflects the first assumption of my work: I believe it is necessary to synthesize all available religious and philosophic knowledge into one system.

There are three reasons for my desire to integrate systems and, in particular, for my interest in philosophic mysticism. The first comes from the present state of the field of Judaic Studies. The tradition we have received from our distinguished predecessors in the field of medieval Judaic Studies is that the key thinkers of the past can be divided into philosophers, mystics, and halakhists; that is, that insofar as one writes medieval Jewish intellectual history, one must deal with philosophy, mysticism, and halakha. (Sometimes exegesis is added as a field, but, except insofar as it is linguistic, it too falls into the above categories.) Moreover, the received attitude is that all of these aspects of medieval Jewish intellectuality are largely separate from one another. And therein lies my sense that something is very much amiss.

In the area of the study of Jewish philosophy, for instance, the standard works trace the "philosophic tradition" from Saadia to Bahya Ibn Pakuda to Maimonides to Crescas and Spinoza, with a side tradition which deals with Isaac Israeli, Ibn Gabirol, etc. All this is quite in order. But this approach completely ignores those thinkers whom students of Jewish mysticism list as their own. Thus Guttmann, in his encyclopedic work on Jewish philosophy, does not deal with Moses de Leon, or with Abraham Abulafia, or with Isaac Luria, or with eighteenth-century

Hasidism. Similarly, the author of the entry "Philosophy" in the *Encyclopedia Judaica*, Baron, and others when dealing with "Jewish philosophy" explicate the ideas of certain thinkers and not others--the list being the "traditional," or received, list. Furthermore, the *issues*, as raised and defined by those who write on the topic of Jewish philosophy, are also determined by a consensus of the scholars, i.e., by a received tradition. Thus the received issues include: revelation vs. reason, creation vs. scientific cosmology, providence vs. free will, God's foreknowledge vs. free will, miracles vs. natural law, proofs for the existence of God, special knowledge (prophecy) vs. general knowledge (epistemology), traditional Jewish ethics and the Golden Mean, biblical-anthropopathic vs. philosophic-abstract language about God (the doctrine of attributes), etc. These thinkers and themes have been the subject of scholarly articles for over one hundred years, and scholarship in this mode has reached a degree of sophistication that borders on the arcane. I, too, have done my share of this type of analysis, having presented two texts from a hitherto unknown area of Jewish culture and having analyzed them as I had been taught. I think I have even made a contribution or two to this type of analysis (the suggestion of "Agent Intelligence" instead of "Active Intellect," the suggestion of an eastern more neoplatonic tradition of Maimonidean interpretation, the suggestion that one speak of "substrate" rather than "Prime Matter" since there might be two Prime Matters, etc.).

However, a very important question remains to be asked of the tradition of scholarship in medieval Jewish philosophy: What did all this intellectualist exercise have to do with religion? What did all the heated argumentation (and it was at least as sharp as the worst of current scholarly exchange) have to do with spirituality? If Jewish philosophy was not just a striving after intellectual clarity, what was it? The same question can be presented in the converse: Did the author of the Zohar have nothing to say on any of the subjects that philosophers dealt with, such that the historians of Jewish philosophy have omitted him entirely from their consideration? Surely Moses de Leon had a doctrine of attributes, a doctrine of creation, of miracles, etc. His thought was no less neoplatonic than that of Ibn Gabirol nor was it less systematic than that of Isaac Israeli. Why, then, is he not considered a "philosopher"? It is my contention that the modern tradition of the study of Jewish philosophy has failed in two respects: It has failed to analyze the spiritual dimension that lies behind (and, indeed, motivates) the philosophic issues of Jewish philosophy, and consequently it has also failed to cast its intellectual net widely enough to encompass other forms of Jewish intellectuality, equally as respectable and as pressing. It is this double failure in the modern study of Jewish philosophy that has led me to a reconsideration of the issues.

As the received tradition of scholarship in medieval Judaic Studies has set off the philosophers from the mystics, it has also set off the mystics from the philosophers. Thus Scholem, surely the crucial figure in the field, deals with the Merkabah and eleventh-century Hasidic literature, Abulafia, the Zohar, Luria, the Sabbatian movement, and Hasidism. However, he completely ignores Maimonides, Isaac Israeli, Crescas, etc. and mentions only in passing the neoplatonic influence of Ibn Gabirol. Similarly, the rapidly proliferating group of books that seek to survey the field or to excerpt texts follow Scholem in the selection of authors who are mystics. The *Encyclopedia Judaica* articles were written by Scholem. Furthermore, the *issues*, as raised and defined by those who write on the topic of Jewish mysticism, are also determined by the consensus of the scholars, i.e., by a received tradition of what the issues are. They include: studies in symbolism, filiation of ideas, studies in mysticism and rabbinic authority, magic and mysticism, mystical Kavvana, Sabbatian studies, and doctrinal work in Hasidism. (I do not mention the amateur books that appear in this field every day.) The thinkers and themes listed here have been the subject of many books and monographs over the past fifty years. I, too, have done my share, having presented two volumes of obscure texts and having explicated them as best I could. I think I have even made a contribution or two to this type of analysis (the explicative presentation of original texts in translation, the subsuming of mysticism under the rubric of spirituality, the raising of history-of-religions type questions with respect to these texts, and the freeing of the understanding of the mystical tradition from the chronological bounds of its previous presentation).

However, a very important question remains to be asked of the tradition of scholarship in medieval Jewish mysticism: After the manuscripts have been accounted for and the symbol systems expounded, how did all this relate to mind? How did the mythic structures which evolved within these various traditions relate to the prevalent philosophic and physical worldviews?

Did Moses de Leon know nothing of Maimonides, or not take him seriously? What was Gikatilia's view of providence vs. free will? The question can also be presented in the converse: If the heartbeat of both the philosophic and the mystical systems is religious awareness, did philosophers have nothing to say which might be called "mystical," such that historians of Jewish mysticism have omitted reference to them? Surely, Spinoza had something to say about the experience of God. Surely Maimonides knew that Kavvana in prayer produced states of religious awareness that had to figure into his system. These men are not less "mystical" for their not being on the approved list of mystics. It is my contention that the modern tradition of the study of Jewish mysticism, like the modern tradition of the study of Jewish philosophy, has failed in two respects: It has failed to analyze the response that Jewish mysticism offered to Jewish philosophy and, as a result, it has failed to cast its intellectual net widely enough to encompass other forms of Jewish spirituality, equally as respectable and equally as pressing. It is this double failure in the modern study of Jewish mysticism that has also led me to a reconsideration of the issues.

Happily, in calling for an examination of the mystical dimension of Jewish philosophy and the philosophic dimension of Jewish mysticism, I am not alone. French scholarship in Islamic Studies has been doing this for a long time. Thus Madkour drew attention to al-Farabi's "*mysticisme intellectualiste*" already in 1936 and Corbin drew attention to the philosophic dimension of Islamic theosophy in a series of articles dealing primarily with Shi'ite mysticism. My beloved teacher, Professor Vajda, in 1947, called attention to this issue and has continued to publish articles and books on the intersection of these fields. Margoliouth once published a preliminary study of the influence of Maimonides on the Zohar. And Wijnhoven, in his recent bibliographic survey of Jewish mysticism, has followed this lead and listed Saadia and Maimonides in his bibliography. There are others, too (Werblowsky, S. Heller-Wilensky, etc.). I have also done my share in previously published work dealing with Maimonides and a fifteenth-century Yemenite figure.

The second reason for my interest in the topic of philosophic mysticism comes from a simple reading of the texts. Maimonides, in III:51 of the *Guide*, states his phenomenology quite clearly. He also states it elsewhere, e.g., in his phenomenology of prophecy, in his view of the Nazir, etc. Similarly, the conflict in Spinoza between reason and love of God, at least

as analyzed by Wolfson, points clearly in the direction of an
intersection of the experiential and the rational. On the other
side of the issue, students of non-Jewish mysticism find the
intellectualism of the Zohar preposterous. Since there are well-
known simple techniques for inducing mystical states, all the
structure of the Zohar seems superfluous. And, a fortiori for
Luria. Furthermore, a simple reading of the *Tanya* reveals strong
roots in Maimonides. This is not simply harmonistic exegesis;
it is integral to the author's worldview. Also, Abraham Abulafia
spent a great deal of time writing a three-volume commentary on
the *Guide*, integrating Maimonides' view into his own cosmology.
No clear connection between Abulafia's techniques and his theology exists, and yet a simple reading of the texts shows that he
considered himself a Maimonidean, i.e., a philosophic mystic.

Third, my interest in philosophic mysticism stems from
a reading of Heschel. Heschel's view is that religious experience precedes religious knowledge, and he cites both Maimonides
and Hasidic texts to prove his point. He also wrote a philosophic mystical biography of Maimonides. I personally agree,
for as I see it, personal awareness of God logically precedes
theological reflection. Personal religious experience is, as I
understand it, the prerequisite for any theology which is not
mere manipulation of ideas. Conversely, the art of theology is
in making the words and ideas we use consonant with the personal religious awareness with which we live. Or, put another
way, loyalty to personal spiritual awarenesses is the directive,
and corrective, influence in theology. Thus the issue of philosophic mysticism has, for me, theological as well as scholarly
interest.

This, then, is what I am doing--articulating as carefully
as I can something of the intersection of mind and religious
experience, of philosophy and mysticism. I do this because I
sense an incompleteness, indeed a distortion, in most modern
scholarship in these areas; because the texts impose it on me;
and because I am theologically committed to the primacy of
spiritual awareness over mind and heart; i.e., to the primacy
of spiritual consciousness over thought and symbol.

II

There are, of course, other problems I could attack. For
instance, we need a good *Sitz-im-Leben* study of Maimonides, his
son Abraham, and Moses of Leon; studies on the relationship between Sufism and "prophetic Kabbalism" and between Shi'ite and

Zoharic theosophy, on the hellenistic roots of Merkabah mysticism; and more work on the nonaverroesian interpretation of Maimonides.

Perhaps the two most exciting ideas that need extended study are: (1) The history of Maimonides' thought as it was read and interpreted by serious Jews through the ages needs to be examined. Such a study might begin with his translators but would also include such figures as Abulafia, the Yemenites, his son Abraham, Moses de Leon, etc. In addition it would include such modern figures as Geiger, H. Cohen, Ahad Ha'am, Kaplan, S.R. Hirsch, Hartman, etc. And, finally, it would include the popular hagiographic traditions about Maimonides, including the one that generated the well-known portrait of him. (2) The whole area of popular medieval Jewish culture has to be reexamined after Goitein is finished with his work. There, questions drawn from contemporary anthropological method need to be asked. For example, concerning patterns of language: How does one tell a joke from an insult? What is considered trivial speech? The use of jargons vs. Hebrew. And how does one use stereotypic "religious" phrases? Concerning patterns of daily living: Who eats what when (over and above *kashrut*)? Why? What does one "not have time for"? What were the attitudes toward money, specifically toward taxes, charity, and inheritance? And what were the attitudes toward: marriage, sexual relations, manhood/womanhood, and childhood/adulthood? Concerning patterns of entering and leaving sacred spaces and time, one must study the life-cycle, holidays synagogue, school, and court. And one must study heroes and models: for adults, for children (education); and popular hopes: this-worldly, messianic, and other-worldly.

For myself, the cultural-anthropological study has only intellectual interest while the study of the Maimonidean tradition seems to me to be premature since one of its main motifs is the relationship between philosophy and religion. The explication of the tradition of philosophic mysticism, then, precedes the explication of the general Maimonidean tradition.

III

Given my scholarly and theological interest in the topic of philosophic mysticism, and my conscious choice of it as the focus for my work, three additional assumptions need to be specified. First, it is my view that, in premedieval literature, we simply do not know enough about the relationship between general thought and religion to draw coherent conclusions. For one thing, the literature is composed largely of anonymous compilations and not of the works of single authors. For another, the literature for the biblical and intertestamental period is far too sparse for anything more than overgeneralizations, while the rabbinic literature is only now being analyzed by the Neusner school for its intellectual worldview. Once we understand more clearly the worldview of the Mishna, the Talmuds, and the midrashim, we will be able to ask: What is the relationship between each of these intellectually coherent worldviews and the religious experiences of the age as reflected in such literature as the liturgy, Sefer Yeṣira, Pirkei Heikhalot, and such pericopae in the legal and midrashic literature as speak of religious experience? At the moment, however, such questions are premature.

Second, the centrality of Maimonides requires that we study his works first. Let me explain. The intersection of systematic mind and deeply felt religious experience will, in my opinion, first be evident when we study a body of literature written by one person (or a small group of contemporaries) who has both a clearly establishable view of general reality, one that possesses some system, and a clearly establishable phenomenology of religious experience. Not even all medieval Jewish philosophers and mystics meet these criteria. Thus Saadia has a systematic general worldview but not, as I recall, a systematic phenomenology of religious experience. The same holds true for Isaac Israeli (whose work is anyway too fragmentary). The Hasidei Ashkenaz have a religious phenomenology and some rudimentary theology, but I do not recall evidence of a clear systematic general worldview. Perhaps Bahya Ibn Pakuda qualifies. Beyond a doubt, though, the key figure is Maimonides, who is really the first to attempt a systematic general worldview (including a cosmology, an epistemology, etc.) as well as a systematic phenomenology of religious experience (doctrine of prophecy, piety, sagacity, etc.). This he articulates in all of his works: *Commentary to the Mishna*, *Mishne Torah*, and of course, *Guide of the Perplexed*. I must add that, even if Maimonides were not the first to do this, and even if his exposition were not so lucid, it is the actual case that in medieval Jewish thought (philosophic as well as mystical) all roads lead to Fustat. Maimonides did become the focus and the funnel for almost all Jewish reflection on the nature of the divine. As Wolfson once said to me, "Work in the post-Maimonidean era! The footnoting is very simple." One of the major methodological assumptions of my work, then, is that while it is motivated by the present, it does not begin there. Furthermore, while it is rooted in the past, it does not begin in the premedieval period and not even in the early medieval period. My work begins with Moses Maimonides because he is the first, the clearest, and the most central figure for this type of study--the intersection of systematic mind and religious experience.

The third additional, major assumption of my work is that we are dealing with an attempt to establish a "unified field theory"--that is, that Maimonides and those who followed him were trying to articulate a system that was coherent and that encompassed as much of human knowledge and experience as possible into one overarching system. This is not a self-evident assumption because life, as we meet it, has many disjunctions and discontinuities. Some things happen to us completely unanticipated from the outside while others well up unexpectedly from our subconscious. The effort to subsume everything into a system, therefore, stretches our understanding of reality. But, if God is one (i.e., simple and logical), then everything must somehow fit together and man must only work at studying reality long enough in order to see the pattern. Whether philosophic mysticism motivated this theological stance or whether man's confidence in his own rational abilities generated this theology is immaterial. In the philosophic mystical tradition, everything (or at least as much as one can account for) must fit and cohere. What one thinks and what one experiences must be inseparably related. Cosmology must relate to religious experience, epistemology must relate to revelation, halakha must have reasons and relate to well-defined principles, language about God must conform to the usual rules of predication, philosophy must relate to piety, and so on. In Maimonides this can be easily shown and I have reason to believe that it can be shown for the author of the Zohar, Abulafia, Spinoza, and the author of the *Tanya*.

These, then, are the four central assumptions of my work: (1) that there is an integral relationship between mind and religious experience, (2) that this relationship can best be analyzed in medieval Jewish literature, (3) that Moses Maimonides is the logical starting point for such an analysis, and (4) that the overriding characteristic of this type of data will be an attempt to synthesize all available religious and philosophic knowledge into one system.

IV

The plan of work now seems quite straightforward. It has three parts. First, Maimonides' cosmology must be established.

This is a topic on which there has been considerable research and the interpretive options are rather well known. The problem centers around the conflict between the biblical and the al-Farabian cosmology, and it is still hotly debated how seriously each of these worldviews was taken by Maimonides. Unless my survey of the literature turns up compelling evidence to the contrary, I expect that the understanding of the first few chapters of the *Mishne Torah*, with the appropriate reservations from Part Two of the *Guide*, will show (1) that there is a willed flow of energy from God, called "emanation" and described metaphorically with such images as light or water-flow; (2) that this willed flow coalesces into a series of spiritual beings each of which is called an "Intelligence"; (3) that these beings contemplate themselves and their immediate superiors in the spiritual chain of being; (4) that the contemplation of a superior generates an inferior in the same chain while the contemplation of self generates either a physical body (actually one of the heavenly spheres with its bodies, etc.) or that such self-contemplation imparts form to (lit., "in-forms") a previously existing substrate such that the sphere and its respective bodies are generated; and (5) that the last of the spiritual beings, called the "Agent Intelligence," in contemplating its superior generates the human intellect and in contemplating itself imparts form to (lit., "in-forms") the substrate of sublunar matter such that the elements and the various combinations of elements into physical objects are generated. These forms, then, actually exist in objects and are put there by the Agent Intelligence. They have counterparts, however, in the Agent Intelligence and in the human intellect. This, then, will be our understanding of Maimonides' cosmology. All is flow. Everything has its proper place. Everything is derived from God. It is monotheistic, al-Farabian, and given the state of astrophysics in the Middle Ages, eminently sensible. I for one think Maimonides took it seriously. It remained only to apply exegesis to the biblical cosmology and to deal with the possibility of an uncreated but ontologically secondary substrate or "Prime Matter(s)."

Second, Maimonides' epistemology must be established. This is a topic on which remarkably little has been written. I don't know why. The subject of how one knows what one knows would seem to be an important one. The reason lies, perhaps, in the fact that the issue of epistemology is usually concealed by the issue of special knowledge (prophecy and revelation) and on these topics a great deal has been written. The complete epistemological system must, however, now be spelled out. Unless my survey of the literature turns up compelling evidence to the contrary, I expect that the understanding of I:68 of the *Guide* and other relevant passages, within the context of Maimonides' cosmology, will show that (1) every object contains its "idea" or "form" which it has received from the Agent Intelligence in the course of its generation; (2) the human intellect contains a matching pattern which it too has received from the Agent Intelligence; (3) through a combination of sense perception, memory, and abstraction, effected by the various external and internal senses, a conception of the "idea" inherent in each object is formed and presented to the intellect for comparison; (4) if there is a match, "truth" is said to have been generated; if not, falsehood; establishing truth, then, is a passing from potential to active knowledge; (5) this process for generating truth is valid for all objects of knowledge, from physical objects up to and including God; and (6) these truths are stored during a person's life, the quantity and quality thereof determining one's level in the World-to-Come. This, then, will be Maimonides' epistemology. Usual and special knowledge flow from the same source. Systematically they are the same, though culturally they have different degrees of authority. Gaining knowledge is a reversal effected by man of the willed flow effected by God. Cosmology and epistemology are two directions along the same chain of being. The task remained only to determine the exact role of the "rational soul," as distinct from the "human intellect," in this process and then to apply exegesis to the relevant biblical passages.

Up to this point I think a scholarly consensus can be counted on though there will be those who differ with me on one point or another. The third task is the establishing of the use of mystical terminology by Maimonides in as many contexts as I can find, but most particularly in the contexts where knowledge and piety overlap. A careful exegesis of III:51 of the *Guide*, together with the relevant passages from the *Mishne Torah* on prophecy, Kavvana, and the Nazir will show, I think, that (1) Maimonides definitely uses terms usually associated with various mystical traditions (although I do not think we will be able to identify which traditions he drew upon); (2) Maimonides uses these terms especially to describe those activities and states which occur after all rational work has been done, i.e., to describe those moments in which truths gathered by the process described above are meditated upon and connected in individual consciousness with God or the numinous; and (3) this intersection of mind and religious experience forms the ultimate model of piety for Maimonides embodied in such terms as "the one who seeks perfection," "Nazir," "*baal teshuva*," "*ḥasid*," etc., and that contrary to the Golden Mean, Maimonides held that such piety was desirable though only for the elite. This argument, then, will show that piety too is part of the overall system of Maimonides. It is the activity par excellence of his cosmology-epistemology. It brings the whole chain of being a full circle and gives unity to the diverse elements of Maimonides' thought and law. It also explains why scholars of very diverse backgrounds saw in Maimonides the paradigm for their work, the mystics emphasizing the postrational activity, the rationalists clinging to the rigorous use of mind in all areas of human endeavor. I fail to see why this argument should not be accepted, but time will tell.

V

A final remark: Classical *Wissenschaft* concerned itself with two tasks: the context of ideas and the flow of the history of ideas. This type of work, embodied most clearly in Wolfson's oeuvre, located and traced ideas from one thinker to another along an intellectual chain. I do not think that such contextualization and filiation of ideas is as relevant a question as it used to be. Maimonides did read certain sources. He tells us so himself. And he did incorporate certain intellectual constructions from those sources. This has been well demonstrated in the last two centuries of scholarship. However, two points need to be made. First, Maimonides maintained a certain distance from these same ideas. He took them seriously because they were all he had and then only when they did not undermine the structure of rabbinic Judaism. Second, Maimonides also existed within the general Islamic and popular Jewish culture of his time. We know, for instance, that his son valued the Sufis very highly (although we do not know which type of Sufism was meant). We know, as Goitein has shown, that Jews were religious in a popular pietistic sense. Maimonides also lived within this milieu. It will be my position, then, that Maimonides' cosmology, epistemology, and religious phenomenology do not need to be traced only to direct borrowings from direct sources. Rather, I maintain that I must show that Maimonides was reworking, in his own way and with his own consistency, either specific philosophic positions or general beliefs and practices. It is the combination of specific and unspecific sources within a search for intellectual and religious consistency that characterizes Maimonides' work. My task as a scholar will be to identify not only the specific sources but the unspecific general ones and then to show how these elements were reworked into a whole. The traditional tasks of contextualization and filiation of ideas may seem less rigorously pursued this way, but the process by which real conclusions about ideas and life are reached will be more closely followed.

Contemporary *Wissenschaft*, by contrast, has been much occupied with the question of how one knows when Maimonides is double-speaking, particularly since he says he will do just that in the Introduction to the *Guide*. I intend to keep this preoccupation to a minimum. It can be a very helpful tool if used judiciously but it should not obscure the overall consistency of Maimonides' system. The preoccupation of classical traditional scholarship--the harmonization of Maimonidean texts particularly along rabbinic lines--is not of interest to me though such harmonizations sometimes yield interesting insights.

Having established this much for Maimonides, the same method of analysis will have to be followed for Abulafia, for the Yemenites, and for Moses de Leon as prototypes, as other ways of seeing the overlap of mind and religious experience in the medieval context. I think such further analysis will be shown to be variations on a theme. If so, then, the book on the history of the general Maimonidean tradition can be written with the added and important dimension of philosophic mysticism.

PART THREE

JUDAISM IN MODERN TIMES

CHAPTER SIX

THE HISTORY OF JUDAISM IN POLAND IN 1750-1815 AND THE SOURCES OF ANTI-MODERNIZATION
An Excursus in Method*

Hillel Levine
Yale University

I

My research concerns itself with the history of Judaism and the fate of Jews in the lands of pre-partition Poland from the second half of the eighteenth century through the Napoleonic invasions. The focus of this work is upon the first experiences of this Jewry with the social, political, and economic forces on the one hand, and modes of consciousness on the other that may be associated with modernization.

To speak of the modernization of Polish Jewry in the eighteenth century is counterintuitive and against historiographic trends. The image before our eyes is of a Jewry defiantly impervious to its environment, insulated from the currents of change allegedly emanating from other areas of Europe, staunch in its otherworldliness, and uncompromising in its adherence to a particularly intense and comprehensive crystallization of rabbinic Judaism. We think of the impressive array of communal, juridical, and educational institutions which expressed this conception of Judaism. Though it has been often noted that these institutions were weakened in this period by tensions from within and interventions from without the Jewish community, that extreme forms of behavior and beliefs including radical asceticism and antinomianism were prevalent, it would be no easy matter to link any of these signs of "breakdown" to the transformations commonly associated with modernization. The transformations are thought to involve an increase in worldly orientation, in which the world of everyday life is experienced as an arena for meaningful and purposeful human action, well-ordered, intrinsically knowable, and therefore manageable. Modernization, thus, has been described by Peter Gay as the "recovery of nerve," or by Clifford Geertz as the "search for the real." Whatever else is taking place among Polish Jews at this time, and even later, it would be difficult to discover indications of an increase in worldly orientations. Do the relatives of Solomon Maimon, as he describes them in his autobiography, show any inclination towards planning and sustained, coordinated, worldly action when they escape to the woods each time a gentry coach passes the toll road over which they have a concession rather than repair the bridge and thereby eliminate the unpleasant encounters with vexed gentry whose vehicles get stuck? In Bialik's *Hamatmid*, one searches in vain to find in the Yeshiva student who has not seen the light of day for many years signs of a religious reorientation from scriptures to the "Book of Nature," from "words" to "works" as worldly sources of spiritual inspiration. Nevertheless, it is precisely this otherworldliness, the social conditions which support it and the systems of meaning against which it reacts that call for careful attention in the study of the Jewish community of Poland, a community which was to be the spawning ground of Jewries and Jewish forms taking root all over the world in the following century.

My interests are both historical and conceptual. The methods I employ are appropriated primarily from two sources: a critical reading of Max Weber infused with and tempered by more recent developments in phenomenological sociology. Weber will be used against Weber. As I shall indicate at a later point, musings upon Judaism and modernization provide more than just another case study for his Sociology of Religion; they represent a major problem for his cultural history of the West and his study of the diffusion of world-transforming rationalism. My efforts to understand the social, structural, and organizational life of Polish Jewry in this period and the way in which it differed from other Jewries are informed by the work on modernization of the school of Dependency Theory. I draw on investigators such as Immanuel Wallerstein who, in pointing to the different patterns and rates of modernization in Eastern and Western Europe, touch upon distinctions significant to Jewish historiography and who, in turn, could strengthen their analyses by paying attention to Jewish participation in the processes which they outline.

In this paper I shall make some general remarks regarding the study of the modernization of Jews and Judaism in this area and period. I will then survey the social context of Poland and beyond that the transformations taking place in Europe. Related to this historical context, I will suggest one indicator of the modernization of consciousness--attitudes toward nature and its empirical investigation. I will review some of the religious spurs to the growth of modern science where it did take place, compare them to developments within Judaism, and against this background examine the positions of some eighteenth-century Polish Jews who advocated the study of science. I will conclude with a call for a broader analysis of Jewish movements and processes which promoted or inhibited modernization.

II

There are few periods in Jewish history which have merited as much scholarly attention as the second half of the eighteenth century, and justly so. For this is a period in which major transformations take place for Jews in Western as well as Eastern Europe. That these two areas of Jewish existence form in this period a salient division, that these transformations are of a somewhat different quality and proceed at a somewhat different rate, has been often suggested. However, a comparative explanation of the divisions and interconnections between East and West is yet to be done.

Research on this period in Eastern Europe has focused primarily on the religious movements and orientations which develop in this period--a great deal of research on Hasidism as continuous with and discontinuous with mystical trends, on the last manifestations of Sabbatianism, most particularly Frankism, and, to a much lesser extent, what is thought to be an East European Haskalah, which is seen as little more than a branch office of the Jewish Enlightenment in the West. But other than to mention political dissolution and an ineffective public discourse on the "Jewish Problem," little has been done to point to the relationships between internal Jewish developments and the history of Poland, and much less to trans-European developments in this period. Even the controversial effort of Gershom Scholem to find connections between Frankism and the Haskalah points to the modern outcome to the West in Moravia. As subtle and nuanced as has been the intellectual history of this period, it may well turn out to be that analyzing ideas rather than relating them to their organizational bases and historical contexts will provide us with less than half of the story.

Research on this period in Western Europe has traced the encounter of Jews and Judaism with European society at the incipient stages of the transformations that we have since come to call modernization. This encounter has been charted along a twisting course between new intellectual orientations generated from within and edicts for reform from without, between new universal conceptions of mankind and exclusive standards which provide the new basis for exclusion of Jews from social intercourse, between assimilation and withdrawal, between the imposition of obligations and the assurances of rights, between unrequited admiration and unfulfilled expectations. Though the historical works on the modernization of Jews and Judaism in the West often present a more balanced and integrated survey of intellectual and social forces, of internal and external developments than those that focus on the East, the combinations of variables are not systematically traced. Historical developments which in their own time have marginal impact and in the long run prove to be altogether ephemeral are not assessed in regard to their historical significances. The better-developed historiography of Western Europe has dominated the thinking in regard to what takes place in the East: developments in the West, such as the Emancipation or Enlightenment, are seen as paradigmatic to the modernization of Jews and Judaism. Insofar as these processes portend changes that do not take place in the East for up to another century, if at all, the discussion of modernization in the East is delayed until the second half of the nineteenth century.

However, this approach does not account for internal and environmental developments in the East which occur simultaneously with or even prior to those developments in the West which have been viewed as reflections of incipient modernization. If the desire for religious convergence is to be related to the modernization of the Jew, then it must be noted that four decades before David Friedlander sheepishly and anonymously proposed conversion to a syncretic Christianity, Jacob Frank unabashedly led hundreds of Jews to the baptismal fonts. Nata Notkin and Rachel Varnhagen, living many miles apart, were contemporaries and had much in common. It is not unlikely that the struggles of Moses Mendelssohn of Dessau to synthesize Jewish faith with philosophic rationalism were influenced by his teacher, Israel of Zamosc, and by the renaissance of medieval Jewish rationalism and religious speculation taking place in that part of Poland in the middle of the eighteenth century, which he mediated to his famous disciple. The efforts of Peter the Great at the beginning of the eighteenth century to impose modernization "from the top" by fiat ultimately had more of an effect on the attitude of Jews to the "rhetoric of reform" decades later when they were absorbed into the Russian empire than did the legislation of Frederick the Great. Such examples calling for synchronic assessment of modernization of Jews and Judaism in Western and Eastern Europe could be multiplied.

The approach to modernization implicit in these studies--in the words of David Friedlander, "What takes place in Berlin in ten years will take place in Glogau in fifteen"--is by no means unique to Jewish historiography. The eminent German historian Leopold von Ranke described modernization as "the spirit of the occident subduing the world." Against this, it has been argued that contact between the West and East preceded the modernizing mission, that it may not have been a "spirit" so much as manufactured goods and, particularly, armaments which extended occidental influence, and that even where modernization had the most significant impact in transforming nature and society, indigenous cultures could hardly be viewed as inert, often surviving quite well the impact of modernization. Nearly a century later, the heterogeneity of the modern world and the anti-Western rhetoric in its most modern sectors as well as developments in the comparative historical sociology of modernization press for a less triumphal and more nuanced study of modernization than von Ranke was prepared to suggest. That the complex intellectual, social and material strands that make up modernity consolidated at a particular time in Western Europe and in North America is a historical fact; that modernization takes place under diverse circumstances and with different outcomes is a truism. The struggle between West and East, modern and traditional, foreign and native, universal and particular, are not settled at any one moment.

This implies a distinction between modernization as a process and modernity as an outcome. Whatever definition or indicator of modernity that we might choose, it should be realized that the modern world as we know it is one and only one outcome of modernization. Another outcome is anti-modernization--an attitude which often calls forth an organizational base to oppose the perceived agenda of modernization, the carriers of modernization, or both. Anti-modernizers seek to restore the *status quo ante*, often restorting to the substance and authority of tradition to oppose specific changes which they perceive, or change itself in principle. We must take seriously those who reject modernization and the terms upon which the modern world presents itself. They cannot be dismissed as primitive or irrational. Quite the contrary, as we shall discover, that rejection of the terms of modernity may be based upon rational considerations and instrumental thinking. However, we are not obliged to take anti-modernizers exclusively on their own terms. The relationship of anti-modernizers to the tradition may be very different than of those who live in a traditional world, unchallenged by an alternate and impinging reality. Similar answers to different questions may not be that similar after all. The reorientation of religious meanings and symbols to oppose secularization, even when successful, as is often the case, leaves religion reoriented. Anti-modernization, both as an individually held attitude and as the basis for mobilizing social action, may have unanticipated consequences, fostering the spread of precisely the traces of modernization in which we are interested.

These assertions regarding modernization--the importance of examining its differential impact rather than origins, of looking at the ways it is perceived and reacted to by those coming under the influence of the modernizing mission including those who vehemently oppose it--have particular significance in relation to Jewish history and the history of Judaism. For in contrast to the civilizations of China, Japan, India, and most of the orbits of Islam in which modernization has been studied, European Jewry was spatially and, to some extent, culturally contiguous with the earliest centers of modernization. As such, Jews had a unique relationship to its processes. They could not remain indifferent to the developments which we associate with modernization. In relation to political and economic developments, they often played a critical role, the assessment of which is still a subject of scholarly debate. Up through the sixteenth century, a point that must be looked at more carefully, the Jews participated in the mediation of the classical and medieval knowledge from which modern science developed. Yet their role was at best reactive, and, in eighteenth-century Poland, largely resistant or indifferent to the processes through whicn, as Alexander Koyré, the historian of science, put it, "human or at least European minds underwent a deep revolution which changed the very framework and patterns of our thinking."[1] Identifying social, structural, and ideational bases of these reactions should lead us to a better understanding of the modernization of Jews and Judaism.

III

How might we assess the position of Polish Jewry in relation to the structural forces of modernization? In regard to this question we must examine two sets of relationships: the Jews within Polish society between the monarchy, the gentry, the burghers and the serfs, and Poland itself within the emerging modern world system, between West and East.

In regard to the domestic political and economic order, it is significant to note that the "Golden Age" of Polish Jewry took place under the conditions of a precocious centralized authority. While Western Europe, not to mention the Muscovy kingdom, was in fact being ruled by feudal brigands, Poland had a strong and effective monarchy, which established the terms for Jewish settlement, terms that were favorable at that. Looked at from a different angle, it might be said that the political dissolution of empires that took place in the West in the twelfth and thirteenth centuries took place in Poland at the end of the sixteenth century. It was only from the 1580s on that Jews began to become what Salo Baron termed in the earlier period the "Serfs of Many Chambers." It is more than coincidental that in the same decade of the last Jagellonian monarchs, The Council of Four Lands took on the form which made it useful in the following years. While representing Jewish interests to central authority, it concerned itself with the situation of the increasing number of Jews living under the whimsical authority of local tyrants. Centralized Jewish governance to some measure increased the security of Jews living under the conditions of political disintegration. This functional organization of Jewish life is matched by the awareness and rational analysis of the political dangers of the *Arenda*, the leasing-out system through which Jews managed the gentry estates, as registered in the frequent edicts the Council issued against this involvement. Nevertheless, the peasant rebellions and massacres of Jews when viewed in retrospect were treated in the same stylized forms of the elegiac literature and these "natural causes" were largely passed over in favor of moralistic theodicies. Jews were managing the "second serfdom" in Poland at the same time that their coreligionists in the West were contributing to the growth of commerce and labor markets, political centralization, capital accumulation, and ultimately modernization.

The way in which Polish Jews helped reconcile the inner contradictions of this Polish feudalism and compensate for its economic shortcomings as the modernization taking place in the West began to have an impact on Poland is a fascinating and complex story.[2] Polish feudalism was not only a means of organizing labor and production. It also gave institutional expression to the deepest romantic sentiments of conservative and Catholic patriarchalism. The lord saw himself as absolute ruler of his estate, which was to be economically self-sufficient and to maintain closed monetary circulation for the primary purpose of generating capital, through the profitable export of grain surplus, so that luxury items, imported from abroad, might be procured. At the same time, the gentry combined physical coercion and economic measures to prevent the serfs from using their surplus grain to obtain goods manufactured off of the estate and thereby do what the gentry viewed as diminishing gentry wealth. The feudal, or what was considered to be the natural, sector of the economy was to be insulated from the commercial sectors involving local markets in order to maintain this economic autarchy.

Between the sixteenth and eighteenth centuries, the gentry worked in a coordinated fashion to ruin the burghers and thereby make ghost towns of cities that had flourished in the Middle Ages. The Jews were integral to this strategy. At first the gentry enabled them to undermine the burgher guilds and cartels by reducing prices. But Jewish commerce could give to the serfs the financial liquidity which the gentry wanted to eliminate. Consequently, the Jews themselves were absorbed into the feudal system to effectively supervise serf labor but also to prevent the Jews from undermining the economic autarchy of the feudal estates by creating markets in which the serfs could participate.

The one crop of Polish feudalism--grain--made the gentry wealthy by supporting the forces of modernization in the West. It provided the food and thereby gave political stability to the new urban masses in countries like England. These masses, who were being displaced by more efficient land utilization policies, such as those represented in the Enclosures Act and by sheep grazing for the incipient cloth industry, provided the markets and labor force for the commercial and industrial revolutions. Polish underdevelopment and backwardness, actively fostered by the gentry in the form of a one-crop feudal agriculture, provided nourishment for development and progress in the West. With the colonial expansion and the early applications of technology to agriculture, Polish grain, that abundant and cheap food supply from the East, ceased to be competitive on world markets. The economic contradictions of Polish feudalism became ever more salient as the economic position of the gentry became more precarious and the serfs became more rebellious and destructive. Again the Jews proved useful to the gentry not only for managerial but also for economic purposes. A growing proportion of the grain of feudal estates, now hard to sell, was used by the gentry in the Propinacja--the manufacture and distribution of grain-based intoxicants, primarily to the serfs. This enterprise proved to be economically useful to the gentry in a variety of ways: it was a more effective means of surplus extraction, it provided the cash supply that had been reduced by the decline of foreign markets, it kept the serfs impoverished, indebted, docile, and essentially drunk, and kept the Jews busy. In the words of an eighteenth-century liberal lord of the modernizing camp, Josef Czartoryski, in his essay "My Opinion on the Principles of Economics," "Without the sales of the Propinacja we would not be able to assure ourselves of a regular income in currency. In our country the vodka distilleries could be called mints because it is only thanks to them that we can hope to sell off our grain in years when there is no famine."[3]

Here we see the important role played by Jews in linking the natural and commercial sectors of the economy and providing the mechanisms by which the economic contradictions inherent to feudalism could be transcended, and when that was no longer possible, at least masked. Through the eighteenth century, as Poland found itself economically and politically, internally and in relation to its neighbors, "on the brink of disaster," the Jews became the target of blame and the victims of violent outbursts. In the Age of Enlightenment and growing liberalism in the West (both equivocal in their own ways in regard to the Jews), there was a noted and tragic resurgence of the blood libel and other medieval forms of attack upon the Jews. The members of Poland's short-lived Enlightenment, Western-oriented and resolved no longer to avert the real dangers confronting the Polish Republic, avoided a direct, sustained, and constructive assessment of its social, political, and economic problems, manifested in and caused by single-crop feudal agriculture. Rather, the "Men of the Enlightenment" indulged in condemning Jews for their involvement in the Propinacja, holding them responsible for its pernicious effects, and even suggesting that Poland's backwardness was attributable to the unproductive economic roles which Jews chose for themselves. Reform measures to make Jews more productive and better citizens were promulgated by Polish modernizers and their successors in the administrations of the annexationist powers. Under these circumstances, it seems plausible that the reactions of most Jews in Poland to this "rhetoric of reform" should have been negative. In opposing the advocates of modernization and their policies, Jews, with a measure of justification,

chose to overlook the alleged differences between the new
"reforms" and the more familiar decrees.

The disorder--political and economic failures--of Poland
in the eighteenth century must be related to international politics as well. Poland stood at the crossroads of East and West,
as a buffer zone between empires; the largest Jewish population
of the late eighteenth century was located between the political,
economic, and cultural spheres of Prussia and Russia. The collusion of those empires plus the Austro-Hungarian empires from
the beginning of the eighteenth century involved, in the words of
Frederick the Great, to keep Poland lethargic. Poland weakened
from within was unable politically or militarily to resist the
designs of any one or combinations of its neighbors. It was sustained by each neighbor to check the avariciousness of the others.
But it was soon realized that it would be more beneficial to
cooperate in carving up Poland as a means of settling each other's
claims. Thereby, the Jewish communities of Poland fell into
different political spheres with the largest part of Polish Jewry
coming under Russian domination. Each administration had its own
policy in regard to Jews, based on past experiences with Jews and
its plans for the newly annexed areas. In each area, Jews were
caught between the conflicting interests of the Annexationists
and the representatives of Polish nationalism, which was revitalized just at the moment when it had the smallest possibility of
realizing political goals.

The alignments between domestic policies, foreign policy,
and positions on modernization were complex and seemingly in conflict, both before and after the partitions. The progressive
Polish gentry, which held up England, France, and Holland as
worthy of emulation, was forced to seek the support of Russia in
strengthening the monarchy and central authority against gentry
prerogative and continued political disorder. After the last
partition, it continued to place its hope for national reunification in Russia. The conservative gentry, on the other hand,
though Slavophilic and most fearful of what was taking place in
the West, rebelled against Russian domination despite Russia's
support of serf labor. Within the field of contradictory political and cultural forces, Polish nationalism, having failed to
save Polish political independence, became increasingly sentimental, traditionalistic, and messianic. The failure of worldly
and political action led to the expression of otherworldly spiritual aspirations. Sarmation culture became the codification of
anti-modernization and otherworldliness. It comes as no surprise

that under these influences and within the complex matrix of political and economic forces, it was all but impossible for Jews to generate planned, sustained, coherent, and coordinated worldly oriented policies. Returning to the example, cited above, of Solomon Maimon's family, it might be argued that they did not repair the bridge not only because of their otherworldly aversion to planning and worldly action but, in addition, because of their opinion that the limited enforceability of their lease did not justify capital outlay for repairs. Moreover, as Maimon implies, despite the issue of their safety, his grandfather's legal bickering and protracted arbitration with the landlord--in true Sarmatian fashion--regarding whose responsibility it was in fact to pay for the repairs, forced upon them the described ad hoc measures. Independent of other Jewish propensities for otherworldliness, the environment of late eighteenth-century Poland provided conditions supportive of otherworldly orientations.

IV

In examining the position of Polish Jews in the second part of the eighteenth century and attempting to account for Jewish reactions to the image and substance of modernization, it has been suggested that early processes of modernization, as they unfolded in other parts of Europe, undermined the failing Polish polity and economy and within those, the already precarious position of Jews; that a selective reading and self-serving assessment made by East European modernizers of developments in the West generated a "rhetoric of reform" which included blame of the Jews for inhibiting the processes of modernization, and thereby evoked a negative reaction among Jews to the modernizing party and, by extension, to the very terms of modernization; that the chaotic social conditions of Poland in this period did not lend plausibility to world-transforming rationalism, the cognitive and motivational bases of modernization, but rather supported an otherworldliness which did not attribute ultimate significance and efficacy to human knowledge and action.

Arthur Lovejoy describes the otherworldly state of mind in the following words:

> The genuinely real and truly good are antithetic in their essential characteristics to anything to be found in man's natural life. . . . The world we now and here know seems to the otherworldly mind to have no substance in it, the objects of sense and even of empirical scientific knowledge are unstable and contingent.[4]

It is this otherworldliness which received expression in Jewish anti-modernization. On the other hand, if we are to find early signs of modernization, what we might look for is a more positive attitude toward "man's natural life" and an elevation of the authority of worldly knowledge attained through the senses and through empirical investigation. Interest in empirical science and an image of nature implying that it is knowable and worthy of knowing would indicate to some extent the plausibility of world-transforming rationalism, a this-worldly orientation which is a concomitant of the "recovery of nerve" and the modernization of consciousness.

Before we can begin to assess attitudes toward nature among eighteenth-century Polish Jews and theories of knowledge which would foster its empirical investigation, we must survey the broader question of the forces that spur the growth of empirical science in general and how these forces related to the situation of Jews and the history of Judaism. While questions of "origins" should be independent of questions of subsequent impact, there may be lingering issues from the point where modern science and the empirical investigation of nature became significant as cultural forces that affected the ways in which they were perceived in a later period. Again it should be indicated that in the sixteenth century, a period about whose importance in the development of empirical science there is some agreement, there were influential Jewish savants whose intellectual orientations did not rule out and moreover provided religious "spurs" for empirical investigation. Rabbi Judah Löw of Prague, commonly known as the Maharal, was more or less a contemporary of Francis Bacon, sharing his emphasis upon observation and disavowal of metaphysics. If one examines the work of Azariah de Rossi or Joseph Solomon Delmedigo, one finds epistemological positions which would disinhibit and even assign religious merit to scientific investigation. Granted that these Jews were not systematic thinkers and that terminological adjustments must be made in eliciting their positions, still it seems rather clear that their positions could have been used as a legitimization of scientific investigation by Jews in subsequent years who were interested in this endeavor. Why, therefore, were Jews seemingly not a part of the "European minds" which underwent "a deep revolution" changing the "framework and patterns of our thinking"?

Before searching for elusive modes of consciousness to explain this problem, demographic and social conditions should be pointed to. In the sixteenth through eighteenth centuries, the main centers of Jewish life were removed from the areas of Northwestern Europe where scientific exploration was most

important. Moreover, contrary to the universalistic claims of
science, it is unlikely that Jews had access to the societies and
academies where it was developing until a relatively late date.
Nevertheless, the lack of participation of Jews calls for
explanation.

     A brief summary of the religious spurs to empirical science and the new orientations which it fostered--this viewed against the issues that became most salient for Jews in this period--should help gauge the admissibility and utility of the empirical investigation of nature to Polish Jews at the end of the eighteenth century. The growth of empirical science, particularly as it developed in the Anglo-American area, has been related to the weakening of the Catholic Church in the late Middle Ages, the Protestant Reformation, and the sectarian wars.[5] Transcendentalism made science both possible and urgent in that the disenchanted cosmos was experienced as suitable for human inquiry and the elimination of indulgences prompted the need for worldly action to improve man's estate. The decline in religious authority freed scientific speculation from religious constraints. The pressure to "save the appearance" decreased and the nonreality of hypotheses as a device to circumvent clashes with church authority could be abandoned. Quite the contrary. The eschewal of otherworldly manipulation such as indulgences and the belief in predestination where Calvinism was influential led to "salvation panic" and eliminated methods for the cure of souls. In addition to "works" as an outer sign of inner merit, the availability of certain knowledge regarding nature reinforced a sense of inner certitude in regard to salvation. Antirationalistic and antitraditional approaches to biblical exegesis emphasized the religious truths available to all. Important shifts in emphasis took place in the modes of knowing and of validating knowledge. Observation was deemed more significant than revealed or traditional knowledge and consensus more binding than the authority of experts. The investigation of God's "works" was viewed with greater enthusiasm than the study of God's "words" as a source of religious knowledge and inspiration. There was awareness of this compatibility between science and Protestantism at an early point. Thomas Sprat, in his 1667 *History of the Royal Society*, compares science to "our Church in its beginning. Both may lay equal claim to the word Reformation . . . they both have taken a like cure . . . passing by the corrupt copies and referring themselves to the perfect originals for their instruction: the one to the Scripture, the other to the large Volume of the Creatures."[6]

Empirical science had other early beginnings, particularly in the Catholic orbit and under Cartesian influences assigning to mathematics a higher function of validation. Moreover, these origins were influenced by diverse currents such as anti-Aristotelianism, neo-Platonism, Hermetic, and even Christian Kabbalistic traditions. For our purpose in assessing the diffusion of and resistance to empirical science among Jews in eighteenth-century Poland, it should suffice to ask: Could Jews have participated in this intellectual enterprise, what religious incentives might there have been, and what problems could scientific investigation have solved?

That there were seemingly few successors for nearly two centuries to the Maharal of Prague in his emphasis upon the study of nature as a source of religious inspiration and on observation as a reliable mode of religious knowledge may be viewed in relation to the different set of historical circumstances to which Jews were responding in this period. The intellectual trend which captured the Jewish community was Kabbalah, particularly in its Lurianic forms. The cosmology which it supported was as "enchanted" as any Jewish cosmology of the postbiblical period could be. Its popularity among Jews, in contrast to that of empirical science, might be attributed to its greater capacity to respond to the Jewish "problem of meaning." Historic memories of the expulsions from Iberia, recurrent persecutions in Poland from the mid-seventeenth century and the disappointment following the Sabbatian debacle made the meaning of Jewish history and God's relationship to Israel the most salient and disturbing questions for many generations of Jews. As empirical science began in the eighteenth century to pose serious challenges to God's Providence, its potential as a source of religious affirmation became particularly dubious. If, to paraphrase Francis Bacon, the spur to empirical scientific investigation was to hear the heavens speak the glories of God and to improve the estate of mankind, there was little in the empirical science of the seventeenth and early eighteenth centuries that held special promise of the latter for Jews. Moreover, some of the epistemological underpinnings of empirical science, including observation as a source of reliable knowledge, consensus as a mode of validation, and the reality of hypothesis as a form of expressing scientific insights, posed, as we shall see, special problems for Judaism.

From the second half of the eighteenth century on, there were scattered autodidacts and small coteries of Jews in Poland interested in empirical science and not oblivious to, though largely critical of, trends in philosophy. It is difficult to assess the number of Jews who maintained a positive orientation to the empirical investigation of nature and sought to popularize scientific knowledge. In this period we hear reports of Jews, even in small towns in Poland, with libraries not limited to classical Jewish shources, and of some who even read European languages. Though this was by no means a mass movement, it is most likely that these autodidacts exceeded in number the score of books which constitute their literary legacy. They encouraged the study of science both as a source of piety and as the basis of some cognitive reconciliation with what they perceived to be the modernizing world. That the acceptance of scientific truth claims might lead to greater social reconciliation with gentile society was to them, in contrast to some of their successors as well as their contemporaries in the West, a more remote and equivocal aspiration.

Particularly those who did not read European languages relied on the medieval Jewish tracts as a primary source of scientific information. However, they were critical of these works or at least the conceptual frameworks in which they were embedded. Their writings were formulated in reaction to perceived deficiencies in medieval Jewish rationalism, the European Enlightenment, and what they knew of the Berlin Haskalah, the prevailing spiritual chaos, particularly residual influences of Sabbatianism, and the rise of Hasidism. Nevertheless, the physico-theological argument, as adumbrated from Montaigne to Voltaire and Diderot and popular in Enlightenment circles, directly or indirectly influenced their writing.

A prevalent reaction to the spiritual confusion of the time seems to have been principled anti-intellectualism and emphasis upon faith rather than knowledge, a reaction which naturally undermined the promotion of empirical science. It was against this background that which might be called cautious modernizers had to peddle their scientific wares.

We gain a sense of this climate of opinion in the writings of Judah Leib Margoliot. He points to those who would argue that since it is amply clear that one cannot know everything, it hardly pays to know anything. Margoliot summarily dismisses this, claiming that because these people have no knowledge they cannot assess its significance.[7] Menahem Mendel Lefin also frequently takes on these anti-intellectual traditionalists trying to expand the imperative to study Torah to include the study of nature. Israel of Zamosc, in the introduction to his rabbinic tract, attacks the self-righteousness of those who renounce the study of science:

> For there are some who are accustomed to scorn any science and knowledge which is obscure to them. . . . And among some of them no advantage or good deed can be found, not Torah nor piety except for the fact that they think that they are inheriting the life of the world to come because they have not tasted the taste of wisdom ever. . . . They hold it as true that that which is primary to bringing us to the life of the world to come is involvement in the study of *Gemarah*.[8]

In supporting the study of science, an expressed motive among these cautious modernizers was national pride. Similar to the presentation of this argument in the Middle Ages, it included an explanation of why the Jews were seemingly backward in this area of knowledge in which they once excelled. As Baruḥ of Shklov states, "for all wisdom and science from the days of Judah have existed for everyone knew it from small ones to adults."[9] Others were prepared to concede that science was "theirs" and "true," that those who maintain that all wisdom is in the Torah are "infantile" and that however superior the Torah is, there is still room to appreciate the wonders of nature.[10] This removal of spheres of knowledge and reality from the influence of religious truth claims may be related to incipient secularization. However, some refused to allow any concession to the claims of gentiles that Jews should know science. For, in the end, this would imply that the Torah was incomplete and how would this differ from the claims made by Christianity against Judaism?[11] Some of the cautious modernizers developed a programmatic dimension to their apologetics, suggesting that the Jews will study science when the gentiles desist from persecuting them. The later Maskilim argued more often that the gentiles would be more tolerant of Jews if Jews would only study science.

Another value to the study of science and the investigation of nature emphasized in the writings of virtually all of the cautious modernizers was that it might reduce the interest in philosophic rationalism. While some admitted to having dabbled in philosophy in their youth, they all considered the study extremely dangerous. Along the same line, Ezekiel Landau praised the mathematical work of Baruḥ of Shklov in that it eliminated the need for Jews to turn to gentile books for this knowledge.[12] Pinhas Elijah Hurvitz cites this as a primary reason for which he compiled his scientific encyclopedia.[13]

Another benefit suggested for the study of science is that it would eliminate the study of Kabbalah. On this motive, however, there was far less agreement. While some, like Lefin, spoke passionately of the many dangers of Kabbalah, others, like Hurvitz, spoke positively of the study of Zohar and encouraged the study of science as part of a larger program to synthesize esoteric knowledge with human investigation and thereby make prophetic powers attainable to its seekers. However, in the wake of Sabbatianism, which was attributed to the immoderate and unqualified study of Kabbalistic texts, concern is expressed by several writers regarding "Hagshamah," a term most often used, particularly in the Middle Ages, for anthropomorphosis, but in this period extended to imply the overconcretization of religious constructs. As Judah Leib Margoliot, who gives qualified approval to the study of Kabbalah for those with the proper spiritual preparedness, states, "But he should be fearful as before a sword not to concretize conceptions of the creator and to stop with his spirit in order not to cast forth his ideas freely and to be presumptuous to investigate in great matters and in miracles."[14]

In the wake of the Maharal of Prague, these cautious modernizers considered the contemplation of nature to be a source of piety. However, two centuries of scientific developments in Europe did not allow them to share his epistemological confidence that proper observation would not undermine traditional verities. Neither could they summarily dismiss scientific hypotheses and findings as based upon uncertainty and the subjectivity of different scientists. Nor were they completely at ease resorting to the Averroistic solution of a double Truth, corresponding in some way to a dual universe, a solution to conflicts between science and faith that the Maharal and medieval religious thinkers could ultimately employ.

Another change in the sixteenth to eighteenth centuries which interfered with the positive reception of empirical science was what may be perceived as the development of a negative attitude toward nature itself. Rather than seeing the hand of God in nature, some came to view nature as that which separated Israel and their father in heaven. This may have been another version of the transcendentalism which was a prerequisite for scientific exploration in Christian Europe, but a version inhospitable to that end. It may have been spurred by Kabbalistic conceptions as well as by the social and political disorder. The diabolic images of nature may have been stimulated by scientific formulations of a mechanistic, determined cosmos in which the God of

Israel and therefore the Jews as God's communicants, had little influence.

On the other hand, viewing nature as immanent with God's glory proved equally inhospitable to empirical science. Notions of some sort of unity between God and nature to be found in the Maharal and later influential among Hasidim made the empirical investigation of nature irrelevant and dangerous, as it could make, in its more extreme forms, exertion and activity in the natural world, even for one's basic needs, unnecessary. This worldly quietism was often complemented by otherworldly activism with magical and messianic dimensions.

While empirical science supported a worldly orientation, these inhibitions on the scientific worldview and belief in natural causation prevented even the scientific enthusiasts among Jews from viewing the world of everyday life as the paramount reality. While human action and initiative could be deemed significant in worldly matters, they could not be conceived of as the only determining factor. The uncertainty in the formulation of boundaries between worldliness and otherworldliness and the modes of human action appropriate to each is illustrated by the following moving and precocious call of Pinhas Elijah Hurvitz:

> For how long should we not do that which is in our power to do that the temple should be built in our days? Does not Zion cry out bitterly and Jerusalem give its voice and no-one pays attention in these generations. Our eyes have seen that all the nations go each one in the name of its country and they fight each one for their land, the land of their forefathers (vaterland) and they risk their lives for it and we are weak and lazy all the time, all this long time. Until when will we not arise to fight also for our holy land and the land of our forefathers. However not with a knife and sword and not with implements of war shall we fight as the other nations, some of which come by chariots, others by horses, but we in the name of God our Lord to learn Torah and do commandments of our God for the sake of His beloved name in order to remove God and the *sheḥinah* from the *galut*.[15]

Ultimately, neither nature nor its study was viewed as all that neutral. Fostering scientific knowledge as a part of the programs of modernizers evoked a new source of Jewish rejection of science. The challenges that the diffusion of empirical science raised--"true" or "untrue," "theirs" or "ours," even "theirs" and "true"--could be and had been dealt with. However, what was particularly dangerous about empirical science as one aspect of the "rhetoric of reform" was that it was no longer relegated to the conceptual and speculative, but had practical implications and it contributed to the undermining of the social position of Jews. As the various programs for the modernization of Jews and Judaism, with all of their contradictions and unfavorable terms, impinged more upon Jews, the anti-modernization responses became more and more vehement. Observation could not be an important mode of knowing insofar as external reality did not render support to innerly perceived Jewish truth claims. Consensus could not be accepted as a mode of scientific validation for Jews who did not experience themselves as part of the universality of mankind who, in the words of Thomas Sprat, "have laid aside their names of distinction and calmly conspired in a mutual agreement of labors and desires."[16]

The cautious modernizers tried to reestablish the basis for Jewish collective life by reformulating the boundaries of the Jewish community that would protect Jews from the insidious and often whimsical measures promulgated in the name of modernization from outside of the Jewish community. At the same time, these cautious modernizers advocated measures to reform Jewish life from within. These often evoked opposition because of the vested interests of Jewish opponents or because of the bolstered authority of precedent and tradition at a time when these were being undermined irreverently from a variety of sources.

These cautious modernizers also attempted to postulate a concept of the natural which could be rendered meaningful by and elucidated through the investigations of empirical science and at the same time would lend support to the truth claims of Judaism and Jewish history. Particularly at stake were notions of God's Providence over Israel. As we have seen, there were certainly earlier efforts to formulate notions of natural causation, even as theodicies. However, the new pressures of the comprehensive truth claims of scientific rationality pressed by absolutist regimes and cultures claiming universal validity promoted notions of natural causation as all-embracing worldviews. Against deists--Jewish and non-Jewish--the cautious modernizers had to defend the plausibility of miracles; against otherworldly activists, cautious modernizers had to circumscribe their possibilities.

V

Three perspectives have been proposed from which the modernization of Jews and Judaism in eighteenth-century Poland should be studied:

1. The differential impact of historical developments inside and outside of Poland on different sectors of the Jewish community.

2. Orientations to the natural and social orders which took on a new salience within the changing historical circumstances.

3. Perceptions of a changing world formed by the earliest encounters with the agents of modernization.

The social position of Jews in this period was increasingly precarious. The high level of consensus on fundamental issues and outward conformity, which had prevailed within rabbinic Judaism for centuries, was now in decline, subverted by a lingering subterranean messianism with varying degrees of antinomianism on the one side and by a rationalism with universalistic claims on the other. The communal structures for social and ideational control decreased in their effectiveness. Along with Polish Jewry's experience of the decline of mighty empires, there was a sense of a new order emerging beyond the perceived chaos. The sources and carriers of information regarding the modern world to small Jewish villages included meandering Jews, Jewish doctors returning from study abroad, merchants, tax collectors, and the soldiers of conquering armies. The image presented was both forbidding and tempting.

The spiritual ferment, as a recent study has indicated, was far greater and more complex than the historiography of the period reflects. The religious climate is described by a contemporary in the following words: "An orchard which has been planted with confusion in which every scholar is in confusion. One says this and one says that in regard to the worship of the Creator, may He be blessed."[17] In trying to make sense of the different types of confusion, it should be realized that we know about only the relatively successful collectivities that emerged out of the masses of Jews in this period--the Frankists, the Hasidim and their different opponents, the cautious modernizers and their spiritual heirs who eventually did constitute an East European Haskalah. The shifting coalitions must be examined as they crystallized around certain beliefs and ideas, took different organizational forms, and maintained different postures toward modernization. In addition to more extreme reactions of rejection or acceptance, we must examine social and intellectual sources of reconciliation. Combining these approaches, we discover new sources of worldliness even in unexpected quarters. There is much work to be done on Frankism and Hasidism as social movements with ideologies which promote varying combinations of worldly and otherworldly orientations among their adherents. The mythological world which Frank may have inhabited and the alleged opportunism of his disciples do not in and of themselves explain how Frankism as a movement attempted to make sense of a changing world. Hasidism, as a fissiparous movement developing over an extended period of time, under diverse political and economic circumstances often a function of rates of modernization in Eastern Europe, taking on different organizational forms and emphasizing different religious modalities, may provide important insights into issues of modernization and anti-modernization.

The outcome of this undertaking rests upon problems of method which do not lend themselves to easy solutions. Divisions between intellectual and social history cannot be narrowed by the mechanical imposition of one upon the other; indigenous and contextual determinants cannot be weighed in any simple fashion. In trying to move beyond the history of thought to the history of thinking, we are pointing to an elusive level of change. In establishing indicators, we must ask about the generalizability of our findings beyond the circles of intellectuals. By choosing our material carefully, searching for extant writings of popularizers, publicists, and homilists, as well as archival material, it may be possible to get a sense of what was plausible in broader circles.

In conclusion, my differences in method and interpretation as well as my great debt to Weber should by now be clear. While I agree with Weber, against Sombart, that the Jews had less than a primary role in generating specific dimensions of the modern world, I cannot agree with the way he reasons this. The historical ineffectuality of Jewish rationalism did not necessarily have to do with Talmudic scholasticism or Jewish punctiliousness in the observance of ritual or the need of Jews to control their overflowing and dangerous "*ressentement*." Here, for reasons that are not easy to comprehend, he overlooks the affinities between rationalism and social order that he was so inclined to emphasize. Given the fragmentary nature of his observations on modern Jewish history and the polemical purposes for which they were made, it may not be fair to say much more. Suffice it to say that in tracing the sources of Jewish anti-modernization and otherworldliness and the emergence of world-transforming rationalism, it is worth remembering Weber's abiding message regarding the importance of integrating the ideal and material, the intellectual and social, in historical explanation.

NOTES TO CHAPTER SIX

*This paper was read at the Max Richter Conversation on the History of Judaism, Brown University, June 23-24, 1980. The author wishes to thank the conveners and participants for many helpful comments. The research was conducted under a research grant from the National Endowment for the Humanities, Ro-00198-80-337.

[1] Alexander Koyré, *From the Closed World to the Infinite Universe* (New York, 1958), p. v.

[2] The analysis of the "second serfdom" in Poland follows the work of Witold Kula, *An Economic Theory of the Feudal System: Toward a Model of the Polish Economy, 1500-1800*, trans. L. Garner (London, 1976).

[3] Ibid., p. 137.

[4] Arthur Lovejoy, *The Great Chain of Being* (Cambridge, Mass., 1973), pp. 25 ff.

[5] This draws upon several important works in the history of science, most particularly Robert K. Merton, *Science, Technology and Society in Seventeenth-Century England* (New York, 1970); Benjamin Nelson, "The Quest for Certitude and the Books of Scripture, Nature and Conscience," in *The Nature of Scientific Discovery*, ed. Owen Gingerich (Washington, D.C., 1975), pp. 355-71.

[6] Thomas Sprat, *History of the Royal Society* (London, 1667), p. 371. Quoted in Yaron Ezrahi, "Science and the Problem of Authority in Democracy," *Transactions of the New York Academy of Sciences* (New York, 1980).

[7] Margoliot, *Bait Midot* (Lyk, 1862), 19b-20a; also Menasse Maillyah, *Alfai Menasse* (Shklov, 1807), p. 16a.

[8] Israel of Zamosc, *Neṣah Yisrael* (Frankfurt/Oder, 1741), p. 3a.

[9] Baruḥ of Shklov, *Kaneh Hamidah* (Shklov, 1784), author's introduction.

[10] Judah Leib Margoliot, *Or Olam* (Nove Dvir, 1763), p. 8a. *Alfai Menasse*, p. 16b.

[11] Israel Löbel, *Even Bohen* (Frankfurt/Oder, 1798), p. 14a.

[12] Baruḥ of Shklov; Haskamah of E. Landau.

[13] Hurvitz, *Sefer Habrit* (Warsaw, 1869), First Introduction.

[14] Margoliot, *Bait Midot*, p. 22b. This warning is repeated by Hasidic masters such as Ḥayim Haikeh of Amdor and Ṣevi Hirsch of Ziditchov.

[15] Hurvitz, p. 107.

[16] Sprat, *The Royal Society*, p. 73. Quoted in Ezrahi.

[17] Mendel Piekaz, *Biyemai Ṣemiḥat Hahassidut* (Tel Aviv, 1979), p. 77.

CHAPTER SEVEN

THE USES OF SOCIAL THEORY IN THE STUDY OF MODERN JUDAISM

Arnold Eisen
Columbia University

Faith in the modern world is a commitment under siege. The armaments of its attackers have long since been identified by sociological theory and confirmed through historical investigation, while the high drama of religion's fall has set the subject and indeed the tone for elegiac poetry from "Dover Beach" to "Sunday Morning." As a student of modern Judaism, then, driven by both personal commitment and intellectual curiosity to understand the contemporary predicament of Jewish faith, I find myself compelled to venture constantly outside the fortress of its defenses. One simply cannot understand the directions taken by modern Jewish thought and institutions unless one grasps--and grasps with rigor and precision--the logic of modernity's attack. Neither, however, can one simply accept without question the relevance of theoretical tools, largely developed out of and for the study of modern Protestantism, to the somewhat different problematic of modern Judaism. As always, Judaism must be studied on its own terms and on terms brought to it from the study of other faiths, each set of terms informing the other. I hope to show in this paper how the social theorists most helpful in understanding modernity's challenge to religion can be used to illuminate the particular situation of modern Judaism.[1]

I

Religions, it seems possible to say in 1980 without fear of contradiction, can never be studied in detachment from the cultures in which, until recently, they played the central role. The historian of religion, if he or she would do more than record and catalogue (and even then), makes use of tools provided by sociological theory on the one hand (e.g., Weber, Durkheim, Marx, Freud and their heirs) and social/cultural anthropology on the other (e.g., Malinowski, Levi-Strauss, Douglas, Turner). Such thinkers, to be sure, do not tell historians what they shall find, but rather suggest where they ought to be looking. In addition,

having found that to which our line of digging has led, we are
helped by theory to make sense of it, through theory's generalization from the sum of past finds and its analysis of the objects
themselves, refined over centuries of study.

Sociologists have tended to emphasize one avenue of
explanation: the relation between religious beliefs, institutional forms, and the socioeconomic-political order. Anthropologists have rather stressed the pivotal function of religion
in the construction of social meanings which these same anthropologists have helped us to decipher. Contemporary theorists,
such as Philip Rieff and Clifford Geertz, tend to draw on both
traditions, having taught us to see their questions as inseparable. This does not mean, however, that the historian of religion can turn to such thinkers for a single and agreed-upon
theory of religion and culture. On the contrary: the significant differences between Rieff and Geertz, to cite only two of
the more important contemporary theorists, alert us to the crucial part which our theories play in determining what we discover with their assistance. If we are to investigate any
modern religion, then, we must pay careful attention at the outset to how religion, culture and modernity are conceived.

Rieff, for example, departs from the current convention
by stressing the essentially normative function of culture. "A
culture survives principally," he stipulates,

> by the power of its institutions to bind and loose men
> in the conduct of their affairs with reasons which sink
> so deep into the self that they become commonly and
> implicitly understood--with that understanding of which
> explicit belief and precise knowledge of externals would
> show outwardly like the tip of an iceberg.

Those "reasons sunk deep into the self," thereby preserving not
only religion but culture, Rieff calls faith: "some compelling
symbolic of self-integrating communal purpose."[2]

One notes, immediately, that culture is not in the first
instance the set of rules, written and unwritten, by which a
society operates, or even the "webs of significance" woven
through and upon what it does together, much less the highest
achievements of its spirit.[3] Culture, before all else, is
"another name for a design of motives directing the self outward,
toward those communal purposes in which alone the self can be
realized and satisfied."[4] The key point is how culture accomplishes this task, through faith--how orders of meaning *and
coercion* conspire to render a particular symbolic, chosen from
the plenitude of possibility, "compelling," so that it is

self-evident that things are done in this way and not that, and, more fundamentally still, seen in this way and not that. Faith accomplishes this task for culture, Rieff explains, through "interdictions": the thousands of 'thou shalt not's' which define us out of infinite possibility by confining us within a circle which we dare not transgress. Interdictions are "negative gifts successfully to resist the strain of observation and the assault of experience,"[5] necessary because both observation and experience testify to the kaleidoscopic variety of what we might do and be at a given moment. If we are to do and be X rather than Y or Z (and only so can humans have identity), culture must both fix boundaries to our experience and provide for our inevitable transgressions.[6] Through such "binding and loosing," meaning—ever-fragile, ever-imposed—is preserved.

Rieff's theory of culture becomes somewhat clearer if we recall a passage from the tradition which is its source. The biblical text (Numbers 13-15) follows its account of the spies' disastrous expedition *la-tur et ha-areṣ*, "to survey the land" of Canaan, with the prescription of fringes for Hebrew garments, *shelo taturu akharei levavkhem ve-akharei 'eineikhem*, "so that they should not go astray by following the many desires of their hearts or the variegated experience of their eyes." The hearts which would taste the new land's milk and honey also yearn for the fleshpots of Egypt, while the eyes which experienced revelation at Sinai have also—and more recently—been awed by Canaan's well-fortified cities. Touring in the experiential domains of others without the benefit of faith's saving blinders would seem to prevent one from ever being at home with one's own God—a key pointer to the specifically modern predicament of Judaism, as we shall see.

Geertz, for his part, offers an "interpretive theory of culture" which stresses the provision of "socially established structures of meaning." Culture is

> a system of inherited conceptions expressed in symbolic forms by means of which men communicate, perpetuate and develop their knowledge about and attitudes toward life.

Religious belief and practice, conceived as a "cultural system,"

> function to synthesize a people's ethos—the tone, character and quality of their life, its moral and aesthetic style and mood—and their world-view—the picture they have of the way things in sheer actuality are, their most comprehensive ideas of order.

The way a group lives is rendered "intellectually reasonable" when shown to be congruent with the group's picture of how things "in sheer actuality are." The worldview, in turn, is rendered "emotionally convincing by being presented as an actual state of affairs peculiarly well arranged to accommodate such a way of life."[7]

Thus, for medieval Jews, ghetto walls lent the doctrine of Jewish chosenness the compelling clarity of the self-evident, while that doctrine in turn made the separations of Jew from Gentile experienced in daily life seem comprehensible and even necessary. Reality and worldview were mutually reinforcing, and the loss of the former with Emancipation made the redefinition of Jewish chosenness perhaps the key issue in modern Jewish thought.

While one should not exaggerate the differences between the two theorists, for each includes in his definitions of religion and culture the factors emphasized by the other, we should note their divergent orientations, which lead to different understandings of religion's contemporary situation. Geertz, first of all, speaks of an "*ethos*" rendered "intellectually reasonable," where Rieff in so many words writes of an *ethic*--a binding and loosing sunk deep and compelling. Geertz's vocabulary is overwhelmingly aesthetic: style, tone, mood, picture, emotionally convincing, image, sentiment. Religious symbols, he writes, "formulate a basic congruence between a particular *style* of life and a specific . . . metaphysic," and his well-known definition of religion calls it "a system of symbols which acts to establish long-lasting *moods and motivations* . . .," etc.[8] This stands in sharp contrast to Rieff's emphasis upon a communal purpose accomplished until now, he insists, by the bonds of obligation, responsibility, character, guilt, shame, etc.: a moral vocabulary essential both to his theory and, that theory holds, to faith. Geertz's functionalist definition, finally, points to the continuing and inevitable role of religion in culture, leading, I think, to the ideas of "religious evolution" and "civil religion" expounded by Robert Bellah.[9] Rieff, however, points to the collapse of faith and, with it, of culture, leaving as the central question whether culture, any more than faith or politics, can survive the loss of authority: "right and proper demands superior to competing immediacies."[10]

If time and space permitted, I would defend a claim which can only be stated here: that Geertz derives his conception of culture and faith from the liberal Protestant tradition which he shares with most of the founding fathers and principal practitioners of the sociology of religion, while Rieff's definitions are rabbinic Jewish to their core. Even leaving that aside, I hope that this excursus into the problem of defining religion and culture has made it clear that one cannot simply turn to social theory for *the* model to be used in the study of religion. As Weber warned, faith-commitments often underlie the approaches which we take to the study of faith, and these must be exposed, not least in Weber's own work. We cannot simply draw upon Weber, then, but must know him well enough to know when his commitments are intruding upon his scholarship. Theories of religion and culture tend, in the nature of the case, to be normative and not merely descriptive. That is not to say that we cannot objectively determine the relative adequacy of varying approaches to a given set of materials. We can. But we must draw from theory critically, and with subtlety.

That caution is all the more necessary when one attempts to investigate modern religion, including Judaism. For Judaism in past ages was confronted by other *religious* cultures. It thus remained within walls which the historian could encompass with a single set of tools, for example Mary Douglas' elucidation of ritual orderings and separations.[11] When the walls break down, however, and the Jewish remnant is struggling with modernity's expanding empire rather than the Czar's, tools useful in understanding religion must be supplemented with those which identify its besiegers. Sociological theory not only does so but places this task at the very center of its concerns.

Here again, however, one finds that the theorists and researchers to whom we turn are deeply divided. While some write quite casually of religion's decline or even demise over the last several centuries, others, relying in part on a different definition of religion, maintain that nothing essential has changed. Whereas the sociologist David Martin once wrote, "You call the chessboard white, I call it black,"[12] Thomas Luckmann, believing that "the transcendence of biological nature by human organisms is fundamentally religious," has argued that religion has not declined but only become "invisible"--retreating, as modernity proceeds, from the public to the private realm.[13] Talcott Parsons, similarly, maintained that in modern industrial society Christian values are diffused ("differentiated") throughout the social system, an evolution which renders specifically religious institutions superfluous but does not make the whole of culture any less religious.[14]

By contrast, the majority of sociologists, who in my view are more faithful to the facts, have concluded with Bryan Wilson and Peter Berger that a process of secularization has occurred. This means, in Berger's words, that "sectors of society and culture are removed from the domination of religious institutions and symbols." Institutions once controlled or swayed by religion, now freed of faith's tutelage, deprive it of its functions. Religion, thus denied the "structures" which lend its claims *prima facie* "plausibility," must scramble to justify, explain and reconcile, in the meantime losing still more ground. Moreover, the sheer variety of beliefs and commitments available for the choosing has relativized faith and thus precluded the imposition of a "compelling symbolic."[15]

The French peasants of Chartres, we might say, once knew their cathedral to be the center and the principal source of richness of their lives. They congregated as a society only inside its walls, learned sacred history from its windows, experienced eternal beauty in its proportions, sanctified their stages on life's way with its sacraments, and never strayed far, physically or otherwise, from its precincts. Eventually, however, in that "sea-change" called modernization, they leave for the city, are thereby loosed from the controls of their community, and confront a multitude of options for their commitment. Faith and its guardians are increasingly peripheral to their lives; polity, economy and society have dispensed by and large with religion. The cathedral is no longer central to its village except as a cultural monument which draws modern tourists accustomed to spying out the terrain of other faiths and bereft, by and large, of their own. Such, in brief, is the sociologists' elegant model of secularization. Up to a point it has proven both accurate and useful, not least in the study of modern Judaism. I have found it so in my own work on American Jewish reinterpretations of the chosen people idea,[16] under pressure of social and intellectual forces which the theory of secularization has helped me to identify.

The model fails to satisfy me entirely, however, for two reasons. First, neither Weber nor Durkheim nor any other of the classical authors in our canon chose to define religion's modern situation in precisely its terms. To employ only this model, therefore, is to leave unexploited the rich harvest of insights contained, say, in Weber's complex concept of rationalization or Freud's theories of ritual and repression. More importantly, the theory of secularization sketched above, while adequate for pointing us to our problem--the lack of "plausibility structures" to support Jewish faith--itself lacks plausibility when pressed to explain the data. It does not have sufficient specificity to explain the changed relation of self to society and culture which to me is the most essential factor in the contemporary Jewish situation.

In sum, then, the road is by no means cleared for the use of social theory in the study of modern Judaism, a task which I find urgent. If we are to snare any quarry at all with our tangle of theories and data, and not be snared by it instead, the first task is to clear a methodological path, undertaken and carved out with the specific materials of modern Judaism in mind.

II

Turning to those materials, we find that our task is made somewhat easier by a marked inadequacy in modern Jewish thought to which Nathan Rotenstreich has called attention. "Jewish thought," he writes,

> has been preoccupied almost exclusively with systems of ideas. Hardly any note was taken of living patterns of culture, living problems, concrete circumstances. The image of the modern world, however, is shaped by ideas incarnated in living patterns of culture; by ideas in action, by ideas which play a regulative role in everyday life. This aspect of the modern world has yet to be confronted by modern Jewish thought.[17]

The degree of exaggeration and patent Zionist bias of that critique do not mitigate its substantial accuracy. The fact is that while numerous Jewish thinkers have reacted to Kant and Hegel, none among the religious thinkers has confronted Karl Marx or, more importantly, the challenge posed to religion by his sociological reductionism. Freud's remapping of the mind, similarly, has reshaped both our understanding of religion and the very patterns of our relations to self and others. Yet Freud and his challenge to religion remain entirely undiscussed by Jewish thinkers with the single exception of Richard Rubenstein. The notions of history which, as Van Harvey has shown, are now principal elements of the "furniture of our minds" and as such constitute a central problematic of modern Protestant thought,[18] hardly figure in Jewish religious thought since the middle of the last century. Finally, science--in Weber's words "the most important fraction of the process of intellectualization" which culminates in modern "disenchantment,"[19] and certainly a defining characteristic of the age which challenges faith fundamentally--has yet to be confronted by Jewish thought of any persuasion.

The harmonizations of Hirsch's "*torah im derekh ereṣ*"[20] or Soloveitchik's Adams I and II[21] hardly constitute a serious coming to terms. To that extent "living problems and concrete circumstances are ignored," and the relation between Jewish thought and sociological theory discussed above is greatly clarified: for, on this level, there is no relation, except of course if we ask *why* there is none.

Rotenstreich, attempting to explain the phenomenon to which he called attention, notes the central role of *halakha* both as "the crystallized expression" of traditional Judaism and as the issue which perhaps looms largest in modern Jewish thought. What this means, amplifying Rotenstreich's point for our purposes, is that to a significant degree Judaism appears locked in a debate internal to its own *bet midrash*, albeit one necessitated and influenced by a pounding on the door and an altered landscape visible through the windows. One should not underestimate the extent to which the debate is internal, addressing issues which in Judaism are perennial: the purpose of the commandments, morality and law, reason and revelation, the meaning of messiah and exile, Israel's role among the nations.

Moreover, the pounding on the door--those challenges posed to Jewish belief and practice by, for example, Hegel's historicist reading of religion, particularly Judaism, or by Kant's scruples about heteronomous morality--can be seen as part of an ongoing dialogue with the outside rather than as something radically new. One learns to live with pounding on the door, after a while. Maimonides had his Islamic Aristotelians, the rabbis of the Talmud had their Paul; so Krochmal had his contemporaries, to whom he responded imaginatively but in a quite traditional fashion.[22]

The altered social landscape, which disclosed the prospect of participation in a gentile society and offered personal acquaintance with that society's religious forms, certainly had an enormous effect. It provoked the reforms and counterreforms which defined the emergent Judaisms of the West organizationally and, to some extent, doctrinally. Jewish observance had to be dressed up, so as not to clash with the reigning aesthetics of faith, and *halakha* had to be repudiated, altered or defended, depending on one's sensitivity to the prevailing Kantianism and, more importantly, on the desire for social integration. Yet these too were internal issues to some degree. Orthodoxy itself dressed up in Western decorum, and fought a battle on the issue with Hasidism, while the amendment of *halakha* is far from a new issue in Judaism, or one exclusively forced upon Jews from the outside.

I do not mean to minimize the importance of these developments. My point is only that if they constituted the whole of the modern Jewish situation, we would not need special recourse to the social theorists' work on modernity, except for the concept of plausibility structures. Sociological researches into acculturation, valid for any culture in any period, would be far more to the point. The largely internal developments, however, are not the whole--far from it. One needs social theory, then, to make sense of a good deal which is said and done, and, even more, of what is not.

A glance at the work which set the agenda for much of modern Jewish thought--Spinoza's *Tractatus*--or the work with which modern Jewish thought in the West arguably began--Mendelssohn's *Jerusalem*--reveals that Jewish thought in the modern period, because of the new predicament of Jewry in the modern period, has set two primary tasks for itself. It has sought to describe a social/political order in which Jews could find a legitimate place, and to conceive a Judaism suitable to that new order. The first task, quite often, was given primacy, while social theory and more strictly religious thought are inextricably intertwined in the accomplishment of both tasks. The non-Jewish sources to which Jewish thinkers turned came to influence not only the reconception of Judaism's role in the modern state but also the reconception of Jewish religion itself. Mendelssohn draws in this manner on Hobbes and Locke, Ahad Ha'am on Spencer and Nietzsche, Buber on Weber and Simmel. The historian of Judaism turns to social theory, if only in order to understand Jewish thinkers who did likewise.

What is more, the two tasks are of such importance to modern Judaism, and so interrelated, that the historian is drawn to define Jewish thought in the modern period more broadly than one might have defined it in previous periods. Without blurring the distinction between the history of the Jews and the history of Judaism, I suggest the following: "sustained reflection by Jews about Jewish faith *and/or* the Jewish community, designed to insure the fruitful continuation of that faith *and/or* that community."[23] A narrower definition reads out of modern Jewish thought much which is essential, and much which is *religious* in the strict sense.

Even this does not exhaust the matter, however, for so far we have remained on that "tip of the iceberg" which Rieff

associated with "explicit belief" and "knowledge of externals."
The fact is that while the reaction of all Western faiths to
modernity has been ambivalent, that of the Jews has been doubly
so. Modernity conferred enormous blessings on Jews even as it
sapped the power of Jewish beliefs and institutions. In the last
generation the ambivalence has become still more pronounced.
Jewish thinkers, for the most part, have sensed vaguely rather
than stated clearly the nature of modernity's challenge. In
addition, one suspects that apologetic concerns--chiefly the
fear of delaying Emancipation by antagonizing non-Jews--prevented
the full measure of Jewish ambivalence from finding expression.
In any event, if one reads the corpus of modern Jewish thought
from, say, Mendelssohn to Soloveitchik, and examines the related
development of Jewish religious institutions, one finds only
oblique and tentative reference to the modern predicament.
Mendelssohn mentions the loss of personal models, Hess glories
in the rise of the nation-state, Hirsch is ambivalent about the
lack of centralized religious authority, Buber decries alienation,
Heschel recognizes technology's dissipation of naive wonderment,
Soloveitchik notes the social isolation of the contemporary man
or faith. Yet the nature of the challenge is never probed very
deeply or systematically, even in Buber and Kaplan. Jewish
responses to modernity remain, for the most part, strategies
devised to meet a challenge which the strategists could but dimly
discern.

The student of modern Judaism, therefore, must draw out
of the Jewish materials a concern to which, often enough, their
"externals" only hint. Since the work described here is near its
beginning, I too can only hint fairly dimly at its direction,
through three examples chosen because they are, perhaps less
obvious than some others which come to mind.

Consider, first, the role of critical reflection in dissipating the meaning, if not the possibility, of symbolic observance. The movements of faith, as Rieff reminds us, depend on
a certain lack of self-consciousness and even repression: recall
Harry Stack Sullivan's dictum that "if you tell people how they
can sublimate, they can't sublimate."[24] Yet modern Judaism,
since Mendelssoh's explanation of ceremonial law as a "symbolic
script," has been attempting to do just that. Mendelssohn
defended what Jews do as Jews as "deeds and practices [designed]
to take the place of symbols without which truth cannot be preserved." By such symbolic actions, he continued, Israel fulfilled its mission, calling "wholesome and unadulterated ideas

of God and His attributes continuously to the attention of mankind."[25] The problem with such a reading of ceremony was quickly perceived by the Reformers, and only redoubled in Hirsch's comprehensive attempt to give specific ideational content to each specific symbol, however obscure. For, first, if one knows that symbol X is meant to teach truth Y, and one no longer believes, with Mendelssohn, that God commanded the symbolic script as well as revealed the truths to which it points, one is free either to alter the script as Geiger did or, like Kaplan, to retain it with an altered meaning. In either case, though, the entire effort is somewhat futile. For reasons clarified and indeed exacerbated by the reflection of thinkers such as Kierkegaard, Nietzsche, Weber, and above all Freud, symbolic action *as such* is difficult for moderns imprisoned in reflection. We find it hard, without self-consciousness, to go through the motions by which a faith-community reminds itself about its faith, and, once self-conscious, we find it inauthentic to enact role-performances which we cannot justify as commanded, even when we know them to be essential to the transmission of the tradition. The added self-consciousness conferred by reflection about the historical and sociological function of ritual in supporting faith does not make things any easier, but quite the contrary.

Or, consider the mission which Mendelssohn would wish our symbolic observances to enact. The very notion of the chosen people presumes a view of self which, in the modern world, has been superseded by a new vision of self called authenticity.[26] Moderns do not, like traditional Jews, seek to grow into a self inherited from their tradition, as it were becoming their parents and grandparents. Neither do they find it authentic to derive the meaning for individual existence from a collective task imposed long ago. Instead authenticity decrees the creation of each self *ex nihilo*, and suffers from what one critic has called the "anxiety of influence," lest an identity be given us rather than fought for and chosen. "Woe to us who live in fatherless times like these," cries the father of Feierberg's protagonist Nachman in his novella *Whither*. The times are fatherless because of a new vision of self; the son Nachman, in Feierberg's words, is unable to accept the thoughts which his father "had inherited from his forefathers so that he too could hand them on down."[27] More than simple disbelief is at stake here. One finds the same inability to accept the traditional vision of self in Berdichevsky's cry for the primacy of the present. He cannot understand how "an entire people, children of Adam all of them, would throw away their living souls just to serve a past, for the sake of the past."[28] It does seem incredible, to the modern consciousness unversed in the inheritance of identity. One cannot simultaneously hold to the view of self depicted in the literature on authenticity and "psychological man" and hope to affirm a tradition which until now, in all its varieties, has insisted on a very different notion of self. Holding the new view, questions of commitment to specific beliefs and practices are decided before they arise, or at the very least rendered problematic. Increasingly, in the modern age, Jewish thinkers have found themselves internalizing the concern for authenticity to a significant degree.

Finally, consider from yet another angle the relation to the past implicit in the belief in Israel's chosenness. I do not mean to exaggerate the distinction between modern future-orientation and premodern traditionalism, though that distinction is crucial. Nor do I want to oversimplify the complexities of our various relations to the past. Nonetheless: as teachers of religion we know that the students whom we teach, if they have any personal experience of religion at all, are likely to know only the "pale, exhausted, scholarly" religions described by Nietzsche.[29] We warn them lest they mistake these for the real thing, and find that much which we would teach them remains opaque because it depends on a view of the past to which they have no access. The finest student of religion whom I have taught at Columbia could not make sense of Weber's threefold conception of authority--rational, charismatic and traditional[30] --because he could not see why the "eternal yesterday" of tradition should command us. A custom of belief observed for a thousand years had no more *prima facie* authority for him than one conceived by committee a week ago. Still more seriously, if the social theorists of modernity are correct, our culture further devalues the past by trying so hard to use it, as a result consuming its artifacts indiscriminately. Nietzsche, followed by Weber, warned about the tendency of our "present age" to

> exhaust all possibilities and to nourish itself
> wretchedly on all cultures. . . . The tremendous
> historical need of our unsatisfied modern cultures,
> the assembling around one of countless other cul-
> tures, the consuming desire for knowledge--what
> does all this point to, if not to the loss of
> myth. . . .[31]

As we students of modern Judaism study the enormous energy which it has devoted to the *Wissenschaft* of Judaism--and, of course, thereby examine ourselves--we should bear in mind Weber's explanation of how the vocation of *Wissenschaft* erodes the meaning of any vocation, religious or scientific. Modernity's many relations to the past, in sum, conspire to deny it authority, a challenge which the various strategies of Reformers, Conservatives, Neo-Orthodox, Neo-Hasidim and Buberians perhaps cannot overcome.

III

At present, such considerations as I have just presented are suggestive and no more. If we are to do more than assemble random insights and apply them to the moment of modern Judaism to which they seem most relevant, the following threefold method is in order.[32]

(1) Using social theory, whether based upon generalization from historical research, as in Weber and Durkheim, or upon observation shown in retrospect to have been especially percipient, as in Nietzsche and Kierkegaard, we can identify component elements of the "modernization of consciousness." The elements must first be identified because, unlike the generally agreed-upon components of modernization (e.g., urbanization, industrialization, the rise of the nation-state, etc.), those concerned with consciousness and the new relation of self to society and culture have not been agreed upon, nor as yet integrated one with another.

(2) Using the lens thus provided by social theory, we can turn to the materials of modern Judaism. We look, first, at Jewish beliefs and institutions as these have been revealed by study to date, and, secondly, at beliefs and institutions revealed to be existent or important only with the help of the new lens. Alternatively, one can begin with the Jewish materials and, suspecting an issue crucial to modern consciousness, turn to theory for elucidation.

(3) The degree of fit between theory and data tests the adequacy of theory, in two ways. We discover how much more or how much more clearly the new lens enables us to see, and we assess the importance of what we come to see or see better within the materials of modern Judaism as a whole. Having done so, we will know better the adequacy of tools developed out of and for the study of another tradition to the study of Judaism, and will be able to refine those tools further for use in future research.

NOTES TO CHAPTER SEVEN

[1] I am indebted to Jacob Neusner for eliciting this essay, and for the many works which have helped me to think these problems through. See especially his *Method and Meaning in Ancient Judaism* (Brown Judaic Studies #10; Missoula, Mont., 1979). The term "social theory" shall be used here to include not only the sociological theory of the past two centuries but works before it (e.g., Plato's *Republic*) or contemporary with it (e.g., anthropological theory) which systematically consider the functioning, real and ideal, of human society and culture.

[2] Philip Rieff, *The Triumph of the Therapeutic: Uses of Faith after Freud* (New York, 1968), pp. 2-5. See also his *Fellow Teachers* (New York, 1972).

[3] Compare Clifford Geertz, "Thick Description: Toward an Interpretive Theory of Culture," in *The Interpretation of Cultures* (New York, 1973).

[4] Rieff, *Triumph*, p. 4.

[5] Rieff, *Teachers*, p. 73.

[6] Rieff's term for the latter is "remission."

[7] Geertz, "Religion as a Cultural System," in *Interpretation*, pp. 87-90.

[8] Ibid. My emphasis.

[9] See the essays collected in *Beyond Belief* (New York, 1970).

[10] Rieff, *Teachers*, p. 22.

[11] See especially *Purity and Danger* (London, 1966) and Neusner, *Method and Meaning*.

[12] David Martin, *The Religious and the Secular* (London, 1969).

[13] Thomas Luckmann, *The Invisible Religion* (New York, 1970).

[14] Talcott Parsons, "Christianity and Modern Industrial Society," in *Sociological Theory, Values and Socio-Cultural Change*, ed. Edward A. Teryakian (New York, 1963). See also Parsons' earlier work, *Structure and Process in Modern Societies* (Glencoe, 1960).

[15] Peter Berger, *The Sacred Canopy* (Garden City, 1969), especially pp. 105-71.

[16] Forthcoming.

[17] Nathan Rotenstreich, "Secularism and Religion in Israel," *Judaism*, Summer 1966, pp. 259-83. See also Jacob Neusner, "What is Normative in Jewish Ethics?" *Judaism*, Winter 1967, pp. 3-20.

[18] Van Harvey, *The Historian and the Believer* (New York, 1969).

[19] Max Weber, "Science as a Vocation," in *From Max Weber*, ed. Hans Gerth and C. Wright Mills (New York, 1969), pp. 138-39.

[20] See especially Samson Raphael Hirsch, *The Nineteen Letters of Ben Uziel* (New York, 1969) and *Horeb* (London, 1962).

[21] Joseph Soloveitchik, "The Lonely Man of Faith," *Tradition*, Summer 1965, pp. 5-67.

[22] See his *Guide of the Perplexed of the Time* [Hebrew] (Waltham, 1961).

[23] See Eliezer Schweid, *A History of Jewish Thought in Modern Times* [Hebrew] (Jerusalem, 1978), p. 7.

[24] Rieff, *Triumph*, p. 5.

[25] Moses Mendelssohn, *Jerusalem* (New York, 1969), pp. 74-90.

[26] See, as a good introduction to the problem, Lionel Trilling, *Sincerity and Authenticity* (London, 1974).

[27] Mordecai Zwi Feierberg, *Whither? and Other Stories*, tr. Hillel Halkin (Philadelphia, 1973), pp. 161, 169.

[28] Micah Joseph Berdichevsky, "Past and Present" in *Values: Ten Essays* [Hebrew] (Warsaw, 1899), pp. 53-54.

[29] Friedrich Nietzsche, *The Birth of Tragedy*, tr. Walter Kaufamnn (New York, 1967), p. 111.

[30] Weber, "Politics as a Vocation," in *From Max Weber*, pp. 78-79.

[31] Nietzsche, *Birth*, pp. 135-36.

[32] A parallel effort, of great importance to the study of modern Judaism, is Peter Berger's recent work, *The Heretical Imperative* (Garden City, 1979).

INDEX

Abot deRabbi Natan, 28
Abraham, son of Maimonides, 85, 86
Abravanel, Judah, 67
Abulafia, Abraham, 81, 83, 85, 86, 88, 92
Active Intellect, 82
Agent Intelligence, 82, 90
Aggadah, 75
Ahad Ha'am, 86, 125
Alba Mari b. Joseph Hayarḥi, 80
Albo, Joseph, 69, 76, 80
Alexandria, 64
al-Farabi, 84, 89
Algar, Hamid, xxvii
Alon, Gedalyahu, 13, 24, 28, 35
Amir, A., 35
Amram, Gaon, 58
Anatoli, Jacob, 72, 74
Anatolio, son of Jacob Anatoli, 74
Anglo-American, 107
Anthropologist, 53, 118
Anthropology, 22, 117, 130
Anti-Aristotelianism, 108
Anti-Christian polemics, 77
Anti-Intellectualism, 109
Anti-Maimonideanism, 72
Antinomianism, 114
Apocrypha, 49
Aqiba, R., 36, 39
Archaeologists, xviii
Arenda, 101
Aristotelianism, 64, 66, 67, 71
Aristotle, 65
Art history, 49-52
Attributes (Doctrine of), 82
Aubert, Y., 60
Autodidacts, 108
Averroistic, 111
Avi-Yonah, M., 59

Baal Teshuva, 91
Babylonia, 20
Babylonians, 20
Bacher, W., 35
Bacon, Francis, 106, 108
Balaam, 15, 16
Banton, M., 60
Bar Leon, Abraham, 77
Baron, Salo, 101
Baruch of Shklou, 110, 116
Beer, M., 35, 43
Bellah, Robert, 120
Ben-Amos, Dan, 35
Ben-David, A., 43
Ben David, Joseph, 77
Ben Sirah, 59
Berdichevsky, 127, 131
Berger, Peter, 122, 130, 131
Bergmann, S. H., 79, 80
Berlin Haskalah, 109
Bialok, N., 96
Bible (Hebrew Scriptures), 75, 89
   Anthropopathic language of, 82
   Isaiah, 19, 20, 74
     10:34, 11
   Jeremiah, 15, 20
     chs. 20,21,22,39, 20
   Leviticus, 28
   Numbers, chs. 13-15, 119
   Proverbs 23:25, 9
   See also individual books and New Testament
Biblical exegesis, 107
Biblical and intertestamental period, 86
Bickerman, Elias, xxvi
Billerbeck, P., 59
Biography, 34, 35, 38
Blood libel, 103
Blumenthal, David, ix, xix-xxi, xxvii, 81
Bokser, B. M., xxv, xxvi
Brand, Y., 36, 43
Brocke, M., 58
Buber, M., 125, 126
Buberians, 129
Burger guilds, 102
Burgers, 102

Index

Calvinism, 107
Cartesianism, 108
Catholic Church, 107
Catholicism, 108
Change, nature of, xiv
Charisma, 12
Chartres, 122
Chiat, M. J., 49, 59
China, 100
Christian
    anti-(Christian), polemics, 77
    literature, 45, 49
    prayer, 45
    qabbalistic tradition, 108
Christianity, 110
Cohen, H., 86
Communal leaders, 51
Conservatives, 129
Contemporary predicament, 117
Corbin, 84
Cosmology, 85, 87-90, 108
Council of Four Lands, 101
Counter-reforms, 124
Creation, 82
Creativity, 55
Crescas, 69, 73, 76-77, 81, 83
Culture, 118
Cyprian, 53, 58
Czartoryski, Josef, 103

Davidson, Herbert A., xxvi
Davis, Moshe, 59
Deist, 113
Delmedigo, Joseph Solomon, 106
Delos, 59
Dependency theory, 96
de Rossi, Azariah, 106
Descartes, 71
Dever, William, 11, 28
Diaspora, 50
Diderot, 109
Dimitrovsky, Chaim Zalman, xxvii
Divine Sciences, 4
Divine Will (free), 67

Divine Wisdom, 67
Dogma, 63
Douglas, Mary, 23, 28, 29, 60, 117, 121, 130
Drama, 13
Dura, 59
Durkheim, 117, 122, 129

Ecclesiastes, 69, 72
Education, general, 3, 4
Efodi (Profiat Duran), 80
Eisen, Arnold, ix, xiii, xxi, xxii-xxiii, 117
Elbogen, I., 58, 59
Eliezer, R., 10, 18
Elon, M., 60
Emancipation, 120, 126
Empirical investigation, 106
Empirical science, 106, 107
Enclosures Act, 102
Encyclopedia Judaica, 83
England, 102, 104
Enlightenment, 4, 103, 109
Epistemology, 82, 87, 88, 89, 90
Escape from Jerusalem, 11
Ethics, 82
Excommunication, 9
Exegesis, 81
Ezrachi, Yaron, 116

Feierberg, 127, 131
Feliks, Y., 36, 43
Fellowship meals, 58
Feudalism, 101, 102
Finkelstein, L., 58
Fischel, Henry, 35
Ford, Henry, 6-7
Fraenkel, Yonah, 35, 43
France, 104
Frank, Jacob, 98, 114
Frankism, 97, 115
Frankists, 114
Frederick the Great, 98, 104
Free will, 82, 84
Freud, 117, 122, 123, 127

Index

Friedlander, David, 98, 99
Fringes, 119

Garner, L., 116
Gay, Peter, 95
Geertz, Clifford, 60, 95, 117, 119, 120, 130
Geiger, 86, 127
Gemarah, 110
Gentile, 120, 124
Gershon ben Shlomo, 68
Gershon, father of Gersonides, 68
Gersonides, 68
Gerth, Hans, 130
Ghetto, 120
Gikatilia, 84
Gilson, E., 71, 80
Gingerich, Owen, 116
Ginzberg, H. L., xxvi
Glogau, 99
Gnosticism, xviii
God, 108, 111-112, 113
    existence of, 82
    of Israel, 112, 113
Goitein, S.D., xxvi, xxvii, 86, 91
Golden Mean, 82, 91
Goldschmidt, E. D., 58
Goodblatt, David, ix, xiv, xvi-xvii, xxvi, 31, 43
Graetz, H., 35
Greek polis, 65
Green, W. S., ix, xxv, 35, 43, 58
Guttmann, Julius, 59, 64, 79, 81

Hagshamah, 111
Halakhah, 81, 88, 124
    codification of, 63
Halevy, E. E., 35
Hartmann, D., 86
Ḥasid, 91
Ḥasidei Ashkenaz, 83, 87
Ḥasidim, 114
Ḥasidism, 81, 85, 97, 109, 114, 115
Haskalah
    Berlin 109
    East European, 97, 114
Hayim Haikeh of Amdor, 116

Ḥayyim of Brisk, R., 60
Hegel, 123, 124
Heiler, Friedrich, 45
Heilman, S. C., 48, 59
Heinemann, Joseph, xv, xxv, 58, 59
Heller-Wilensky, S., 84
Hermetic, 108
Heschel, Abraham Joshua, xxvi, 85, 126
Hess, 126
Hillel ben Samuel, 80
Hirsch, S. R., 86, 124, 126, 127, 131
Historian, 6, 14
    of religion, 38
    legal, 53
Historicism, 7, 21
Historicist, 8
History, approaches and types of, 3-29, 32, 34, 49-52, 83
Hobbes, 65, 125
Hoffman, L. A., 46-47, 58
Holland, 104
Holy man, 3, 14
Ḥoni HaMe'agel, 9, 11, 12, 13, 15, 16, 24, 25, 26
Humane studies, 4
Humanities, 3, 4
Hurvitz, Pinhas Elijah, 110, 111, 112, 116

Iberia, 108
Ibn Gabirol, 81, 82, 83
Ibn Pakuda, Baḥya, 81, 87
Ibn Tibbon, Judah, 75
Ibn Tibbon, Moses, 69, 74
Ibn Tibbon, Samuel, 69, 72, 74, 76
Ideas, 123
India, 100
Indulgences, 107
Intention, 55, 83, 84, 90
Islam, 100
Israel, 24, 108, 112, 113
    land of, 19
    people of, 9, 16
Israeli, Isaac, 81, 82, 83, 87

Jacob ben Makir, 75
Jagellonian monarchs, 101

Index   139

Japan, 100
Jerusalem, 9, 10, 17, 18, 19, 20, 112
    inhabitants of, 20
Jesus, 25
Jewish commerce, 102
Jewish community, 113
Jewish culture, popular medieval, 86
Jewish Enlightenment, 97
Jewish magical praxis, 12
Jews, medieval, 120
Jonathan Hacohen of Lunel, 76
Josephus, 11
Joshua, R., 10, 18
Judah Halevi, 67
Judah Löw of Prague, 106

Kabbalah, 63, 111
    Christian, 108
    Lurianic, 108
    prophetic, 85
Kalamic, 64
Kallah, 43
Kant, I., 123, 124
Kantianism, 66
Kaplan, M., 86, 126, 127
Karaite, 79
Katz, Jacob, xxv, xxvii
Khusro I, 39
Kierkegaard, 127, 129
Knowledge (of Scripture), 14, 15
Kosovsky, Moshe, xxv
Koyré, Alexander, 100, 116
Kraabel, A. T., 50
Krauss, S., 59
Krochmal, N., 124, 131
Kula, Witold, 116

Landau, Ezekiel, 110
Law, 67
Lebanon, 19
Lefin, Menahem Mendel, 109, 111
Leibman, Charles S., xxvii
Leon, Moses de, 81, 82, 84, 85, 86, 92
Levi ben Abraham, 69
Levine, Hillel, ix, xiii, xxi-xxii, xxv, xxvii, 95

Levinger, J., 79
Levi-Strauss, 117
Leviticus, 28
Liberalism, 103
Literature, 5, 22
    Christian, 45, 49
    eleventh-century Hasidic, 83
    structuralist interpretation of, 14
Little, D., 60
Liturgy, 87
Löbel, Israel, 116
Locke, 125
Lovejoy, Arthur, 105, 116
Luckmann, Thomas, 121, 130
Luria, Isaac, 81, 83, 85
Lurianic kabbalah, 108

Madkour, 84
Magic, 83
Maimon, Solomon, 96, 105
Maimonidean
    approach and controversy, 72, 74, 85
    interpretation, 82
    tradition, 86
Maimonides, xviii, 40, 41, 64, 67, 69, 71, 72, 73, 76, 80, 81, 83, 84, 85, 86, 87, 88, 89, 90, 91, 124
    cosmology of, 88
    Guide to the Perplexed, 74, 75, 84, 85, 89, 90, 92
        Introduction, 92
        I:68, 90
        III:51, 90
    Mishneh Torah, 89, 90
Malinowski, 117
Manuscripts, 68
Margolioth, Judah Leib, 109, 111, 116
Margoliouth, 84
Martin, David, 121, 130
Marx, 117, 123
Maskilim, 110
Master, of Scripture and of Torah, 15
Matityahu Hayitzhari, 77
Mendelssohn, Moses, 98, 125, 126, 127, 131
Merkabah, 83, 86
Merton, Robert K., 116
Messianism, 114
Metaphysical concepts, 55
Middle Hebrew, 38

Index 141

Midrash, 4, 38, 51, 75
Millgram, Joseph, 58
Mills, C. Wright, 130
Miracle worker, 9, 24, 25
Miracles, 11, 82
Mishnah, 4, 25, 36, 40, 41, 51, 52
    M. Avot, 41
    M. Berakhot, 53-55, 59
        1:1-3:5, 58
        1:3, 59
        1:4, 2:1, 54
        4:4, 58
        5:1, 54
    M. Shabuot 3:8, 3:11, 60
Modern Germany, 64
Modern religion, 121
Modern science, 97, 100
Modernity, 99, 117-131
Modernization, 95-116
Modernizers, cautious, 110, 114
Montaigne, 109
Moravia, 97
Moreshet, 43
Moses of Salerno, 69, 74
Munk, Elie, 58-59
Muscovy, 101
Mystical terminology, 90
Mysticism, 81, 83
Mysticism, philosophical, xix-xx, 81-92
Mystics, 83
Myth, 83

Narrative, 7
Natural, 113
Natural law, 82
Nature, 110, 111, 112
Nazir, 84, 90, 91
Nebuchadnezzar, 20
Nelson, Benjamin, 116
Neo-Hasidim, 129
Neo-Orthodox, 129
Neo-Platonism, 64, 82, 108
Neusner, Jacob, ix, xiii, xiv, xv-xvi, xvii, xxv, xxvi,
    xxvii, 28, 29, 32, 35, 36, 39, 43, 44, 59, 60, 87, 130
New Testament, xviii
    Matthew 6:1-18,22-25, 59
    Luke 18:9-14, 59

Neitzsche, 125, 127, 128, 129, 131
Noah, 16
Notkin, Nata, 98
Noy, Dov, 35

Oath, 9
Origen, 53, 58
Orthodoxy, 124
Ostia, 59

Palestine, 49, 50
Palmer, R., 80
Parson, Talcott, 121, 130
Particularity, 65
Passmore, John, 65, 79
Passover, 76
Patriarchalism, 101
Pearson, Birger A., xxvi
Peter the Great, 98
Petuchowski, J. J., 58
Philo, xviii, 64
Philology, 11
Philosophers, 63, 83
Philosophical concepts of Rabbinic thought, 55
Philosophical mysticism, xix-xx, 81-92
Philosophy, 63-92
    abstract language of, 82
    Jewish, xviii-xxi, 5, 63
    Medieval, 71
Phylacteries, 49, 51, 60
Physico-theological argument, 109
Picasso, Pablo, xxi
Piekaz, Mendel, 116
Piety, 87
Pines, S., 79
Pirkei Heikhalot, 87
Pirqa, 43
Plato, 66, 67, 130
Poland, 95-116
    grain of, 102
    Jewry of, 95, 96
    modernizers of, 103
Politics, 26
Posek, 63
Power, 55

Index

Prayer, 45-60
Predestination, 107
Priene, 59
Priests, 51
Prime Matter, 82, 89
Prophecy, 82, 87, 90
Propinacja, 103
Protestant Reformation, 107
Protestantism, 107, 117
Providence, 82, 84, 113
Prussia, 104
Pseudepigrapha, 49

Quietism, 112
Qumran, 49
    Damascus Document (CDC 6), 59
    literature of, 59
    Manual of Discipline (IQSl), 59
    XQ phyl 1-4, 51

Rabbi, role, nature, and authority of, 9, 13, 14, 15, 63, 65, 83
Rabbinic Judaism, 95
Rabbinic philosophic attitude, 55
Rationalism, 114, 115
Ravitzky, Avi, ix, xiv, xviii-xix, xxv, 63, 79, 80
Reason, 82
Reformation, 107
Reformers, 127, 129
Reforms, 124
Reiff, Philip, 118, 120, 121, 125, 126, 130
Religion, 6
Religious
    experience, 85, 87, 88
    knowledge, 85
    studies, 3, 4
Revelation, 82, 88
Richter, Max, ix
Ritual, 45, 46, 49, 53, 55, 115
Roman Emperor, 14
Roman Palestine, 50, 52
Rome, 19
Rosenberg, S., 79, 80
Rosh Yeshiva/Resh Metivta, 43
Rotenstreich, Nathan, 123, 124, 130
Rubenstein, Richard, 123
Russia, 98, 104

Saadia, 81, 84, 87
Sabbatian movement, 83
Sabbatianism, 97, 108, 109, 111
Sacred space, 86
Sage, 13, 14
Saldarini, Anthony J., xxv
Sandmel, 39, 43
Sarason, R. S., 58
Sardis, 59
Sarmation, 104, 105
Sarna, N. M., xxvi
Schäfer, Peter, 35, 43
Scholem, Gershom, 83, 97
Schorske, Carl, 5, 6, 7, 20, 28
Schweid, Eliezer, 131
Schwied, A., 79
Science, 111, 112
Scientific cosmology, 82
Scripture, 15, 20, 51
    knowledge of, 14, 15
Scythopolis, 50
Secularization, 122
Sefer Yeṣira, 87
Sepphoris, 50
Serf, 102, 103, 104
Serfdom, 101, 116
Sermon, 65, 76
Sermonetta, G. B., 79, 80
Ṣevi Hirsch of Ziditchov, 116
Shema', 48, 54
Shi'ite, 84
    theosophy, 86
Simeon b. Shataḥ, 9, 12, 16, 24
Simmel, 125
Sirat, C., 80
Sixteenth century, 100
Slavophilic, 104
Smart, H. R., 79
Smith, C. W. F., 59
Smith, Howard, ix
Smith, Jonathan Z., 28
Smith, Morton, xxvi, 50, 59
Social theory, 130

Index

Sociological theory, 117-131
Sociologists, 118
Sociology; of religion, 96
Sokoloff, 43
Solomon, 19
Soloveitchik, J. B., 60, 124, 126, 131
Sombart, 115
Song of Songs, 69
Spain, medieval, 64
Spencer, 125
Sperber, Daniel, 35, 39, 43
Spinoza, 64, 71, 81, 84, 88
    Tractatus of, 125
Spiritual consciousness, 85
Sprat, Thomas, 107, 113, 116
Stobi, 59
Stories, 7-29, 33, 35-36
Strack, H. L., 59
Structuralism, 7, 8, 14, 21, 22
Substrate, 82
Sufis, 91
Sufism, 85
Sullivan, Harry Stack, 126
Symbolism, 83
Symbols, 83, 85
Synagogue, 49, 50, 52
    archeological remains of, 49-52
    staff or officers of, 51

Talmon, Shemaryahu, xxvi
Talmud, 4, 31-44, 51
    Babylonian, B. Ber. 16b-17a, 58
    Palestinian, Y. Ber. 4:2, 7d, 58
    scholasticism of, 115
Talmudic history, 31-44
Tanya, 85, 88
Tatarkiewicz, L., 80
Tcherikover, Victor, xxvi
Teaching, 51
Tefillah, 54
Temple, 10, 19, 20, 112
Temple Mount, 9
Tertullian, 53, 58
Teryakian, Edward A., 130
Tetracomia, 50

Textual analysis, 6
Texts, 3, 7
Theology, 4
Theosophy, 86
Thought, 85
Thurman, Arnold, 60
Tibbonides, 74, 75
Tiberias, 50
Torah, 13, 15, 18, 19, 24, 25, 49, 112
Tosefta, 51
    T. Ber.
        1:1-10, 58
        1:2,4, 59
        3:7, 58
Towner, W. S., xv, xxv
Trachtenberg, Joshua, 12, 28
Transcendentalism, 107, 111
Trilling, Lionel, 131
Turner, 117
Twersky, Isadore, xxv, xxvi
Twiss, S. B., 60

Universality, 65
Urbach, E. E., 39, 43

Vajda, 84
Van Harvey, 123, 130
Van Woodward, C., xxvi
Varnhagen, Rachel, 98
Vermes, Geza, xv, xxv
Vespasian, 10-14, 17-20, 24
Voltaire, 109
von Ranke, Leopold, 99

Wallerstein, Immanuel, 96
Weber, Max, xxi, 96, 115, 117, 121, 122, 123, 125, 127, 128, 129, 130
Weiss, I. H., 35
Werblowsky, 84
Whitehead, A. N., 66, 79
Wijnhoven, 84
Wilson, Bryan, 122
Winston, David, ix
Wissenschaft des Judentums, 68, 128
Wolfson, H. A., 79, 80, 85, 87, 91

Wonder-workers, 25
Wonder-working, 26
Words, 55
World-to-Come, 90, 110
Wuellner, Wilhelm, ix

Yadin, Y., 51, 60
Yavneh, 10, 13, 18, 19
Yehuda ben Shlomo, 68
Yemenites, 86, 92
Yeshiva, 96
Yoḥanan b. Zakkai, R., 10-20, 24, 26, 35

Zahavy, Tzvee, ix, xiv, xvii-xviii, 45
Zamosc, Israel of, 98, 109
Zeraḥyah Halevi, 77
Zeraḥyah Hen, 74, 80
Zion, 112
Zionist, 123
Zohar, 82, 83, 84, 85, 88, 111
    theosophy of, 86

		DATE DUE	

```
BM      History of Judaism the next ten years / by
30      Baruch M. Bokser. -- Chico, CA : Scholars
H57     Press, c1980.
1980
           xxvii, 147 p. ; 23 cm. (Brown Judaic
        studies ; no. 21)
           Papers presented at the 5th Max Richter
        Conversation on the History of Judaism.
20360      Includes bibliographical references & index.

           1. Judaism--Historiography--Congresses.
        2. Philosophy, Jewish--Congresses. 3. Philo-
        sophy, Medieval--   Congresses. I. Bokser,
        Baruch M.  II.      Brown University, III.
        Title. IV. Series.
```